The How-To Book of

CATHOLIC DEVOTIONS

The How-To Book of CATHOLIC DEVOTIONS

Everything You Need to Know But No One Ever Taught You

Mike Aquilina
and
Regis J. Flaherty

Our Sunday Visitor Publishing Division
Our Sunday Visitor, Inc.
Huntington, Indiana 46750

Our Sunday Visitor Publishing Division
Our Sunday Visitor, Inc.
200 Noll Plaza
Huntington, IN 46750

LCCCN: 99-75032
ISBN: 0-87973-415-9

Cover design by Tyler Ottinger
Edited by Lisa Grote
PRINTED IN THE UNITED STATES OF AMERICA

Table of Contents

Introduction / 9

A Beginning / 13
    How to Pray

Catholic Prayers / 18
    How to Pray the Sign of the Cross / 18
    How to Pray the Basic Prayers: Our Father, Hail
        Mary, Glory Be / 23
    How to Make a Morning Offering / 29
    How to Pray at Mealtimes / 33
    How to Make an Act of Faith / 35
    How to Make an Act of Hope / 39
    How to Make an Act of Charity (Love) / 43
    How to Pray the Jesus Prayer / 49

A Tradition of Prayer / 52
    How to Make a Prayer of Thanksgiving / 52
    How to Read the Bible / 55
    How to Practice "Mental Prayer" / 59
    How to Meditate / 65
    How to Pray an Aspiration (Ejaculation) / 71
    How to Pray to the Saints / 76
    How to Pray to Angels / 82
    How to Observe First Fridays and First
        Saturdays / 86
    How to Help the Dying / 90
    How to Pray for the Dead / 94

Praying With Mary / 99
    How to Pray to Mary / 99
    How to Pray the Rosary / 107
    How to Pray the Angelus and Other Noonday
        Prayers / 116

Penitential Devotions / 119

How to Examine Your Conscience / 119
How to Go to Confession
   (Sacrament of Reconciliation and Penance) / 124
How to "Offer It Up" / 133
How to Fast / 137
How to Spend Your Fridays Like a Catholic / 140
How to Live Lent / 143
How to Make an Act of Contrition / 147

Eucharistic Devotions / 150

How to Pray the Mass / 150
How to Make a Holy Hour / 160
How to Make a Eucharistic "Visit" / 169
How to Keep the Lord's Day Holy / 174

Sacramentals and Blessings / 179

How to Pray With Sacred Images / 179
How to Make a Consecration / 185
How to Make a Pilgrimage to a Holy Place / 195
How to Pray a Novena / 200
How to Pray the Stations of the Cross / 206
How to Use Holy Water / 214
How to Use a Vigil Candle / 218
How to Wear a Scapular / 220
How to Wear a Medal / 227

Living the Faith / 230

How to Make a "Plan of Life" / 230
How to Keep the Presence of God / 234
How to Witness to the Faith / 238
How to Begin Spiritual Direction / 243
How to Do "Spiritual Reading" / 248
How to Study the Faith / 253
How to Pray for the Pope / 258

Where to Learn More / 263

Introduction

Did you ever attend devotions and find you were the only person who had no idea what to do next?

Do you ever meet people who seem to pray as if it's second nature, and wish you could have what they have?

Do you often wish you had words or gestures to tell God what you *really* think and feel?

Do you feel something is missing in your life and suspect it might be prayer?

If you answered yes to one or more of those questions . . . congratulations! You're normal.

You see, it's normal for us to want to pray. God built us that way, just as He built us to hunger for the food that sustains us. But it is sad to say that, because our world isn't all it should be, it's normal for us to be clueless about how to go about this business of prayer. Maybe no one ever bothered to teach us. Maybe we didn't feel like listening when people tried to teach us. Maybe our would-be teachers turned us off from prayer, for one reason or another.

Whatever the reason, we find ourselves, today, longing for something that seems just beyond our reach, yet something that is essential for our lives. The situation can be frustrating. If we were as ill-equipped for eating as we are for prayer, we'd all have starved long ago.

We need to pray. Yet how should we pray? The simple answer is: We should pray as Jesus taught us to pray. For, in Jesus, God became man. He had a body, a soul, a job, a family, a religion, and friends. As both God and man, He held a unique authority on human prayer: He could raise prayers as we do; He could listen as God does.

His friends detected His expertise, and they asked Him what we would ask Him today: "Lord, teach us to pray" (Lk 11:1; Mt 6:9). He responded by teaching them the Lord's Prayer, the Our Father.

But He taught them in other ways as well. He taught them by His example. Jesus' own prayer life was rich and varied. Sometimes He offered formal prayers. We know, for example, that He prayed the Morning Offering of all pious Jews: "Hear, O Israel: The Lord our God, the Lord is one; and you shall love the Lord your God with all your heart, and with all your soul, and with all your mind, and with all your strength" (Mk 12:29). At other times, Jesus prayed more spontaneously, raising heartfelt prayers of thanks (Jn 11:41-42). He often took time to pray alone in silence (Lk 3:21-22, 5:16, 6:12, 11:1). Yet He also prayed together with His friends (Lk 9:18). Jesus fasted, too (Mt 4:2). He read the Scriptures (Lk 4:16-20) and prayed the Psalms (Mk 15:34). He marked holy days, made pilgrimages, and attended liturgy (Jn 7:10-14).

The first Christians followed their Lord in these practices, as have all the subsequent generations of believers. As the Gospel spread beyond Jesus' homeland, Christians adapted the Lord's habits of prayer to their own cultures and needs. Thus, over time, the details have sometimes changed, but the forms of prayer have remained essentially the same and just as effective as ever in their power to heal, bring peace, and draw us closer to God.

Today we call these ways of prayer our "devotions," and this book is all about Catholic devotions as they've developed in the great Tradition. From a wide variety of

10

sources — saints, popes, and ordinary believers like you and me — we have gathered practical advice on how to pray in the many ways that Catholics pray. In each chapter, you'll find this good advice arranged to guide you, step-by-step, through a particular traditional practice.

This is not to say that prayer is merely a technique. No, prayer is a loving conversation. But sometimes conversation proceeds more smoothly with the help of set phrases and even formal declarations. Consider, for example, all the ways in which a husband and wife communicate: formal marriage vows, casual chat, winks across a crowded room, affectionate caresses, and a number of phrases they never tire of repeating.

Our communication with God encompasses a similar range of expressions, set phrases, quiet conversation, gestures such as the Sign of the Cross, and the intimate embrace of the sacraments. Just as a man and woman truly grow in love by repeating "I love you," so we Christians grow in love by repeating the prayers of the Church's great Tradition.

In the pages of this book, you'll find many forms of prayer, and all of them are good. But not all of them will serve the needs of every Christian. It's unlikely that anyone could fruitfully incorporate all these devotions into a normal, everyday life. You need to find balance. You need to find the forms of prayer that suit you and help you to grow. These will vary depending on your temperament, personality, maturity, and season in life.

The ways of prayer are as varied as the ways of family life or professional life; and, like home life and work routines, our ways of prayer may change many times over the course of our lives. There will be seasons when we are especially grateful to God, and seasons when we feel especially sorry for our sins; there will be seasons when we feel God especially near, and times when we can't seem to find Him. There will be times when we need a mother's love, and then we will deepen our Marian devotion.

The important thing is to cultivate a *life of prayer*. For prayer is something living. It is no more a collection of techniques than you are a pile of bones and cells. Prayer is a heart that beats constantly within your soul. Prayer is a voice that raises itself instinctively to God. Prayer is a pair of eyes that see God in every person and every circumstance.

You've read this far because you want to pray. Perhaps you don't feel the desire as intensely as you would like. But at least you *want to want to* pray, and that is enough for God to make a beginning.

Let's begin, then, at the beginning. And let's keep going ever afterward. We have the Lord's assurance that, if we persevere in the ways of prayer, we will live a life that is nothing less than divine.

A Beginning

How to Pray

Beginning to pray — this topic alone could easily consume this entire book. It could, in fact, fill many libraries. Yet, the essential concept of prayer is simple. One classic definition is: "The raising of the mind and heart to God in adoration, thanksgiving, reparation, and petition." Prayer is communication with a God Who loves us. It is important to remember that Christ is the one Who has initiated this communication with us. Prayer is our response to Jesus and His love for us.

Prayer involves mental activity. We turn our *minds* to God. However, it is much deeper than mere thinking. Prayer also is a love embrace of God. It can be vocal or meditative, private or public. It may involve words, whether of a formula or our own. Contemplation of the mystery of God and His goodness and love can also form our prayer.

Daily personal prayer is a gateway to developing a more intimate relationship with God. Set aside a specific time to pray. A specific place can also be helpful, perhaps at church before Our Lord in the tabernacle, or in the solitude of your bedroom, or in some other place that is quiet and as free of distractions as possible. Begin your prayer by an act of the will, placing yourself in God's presence.

Of course, you're always in God's presence; but you're not always aware of it. Make yourself aware of His presence, and greet Him affectionately. Such a greeting is a great way to start any conversation.

As you begin to pray, it can be helpful to have some structured format. Maybe you'll spend part of the time reciting formal prayers from memory or from a good prayer book. Remember, this shouldn't be mindless activity. We should concentrate our thoughts on God and what the words mean and express. The Our Father is a prayer that is easily memorized, yet it holds a treasure of meaning and intention for the person who uses it meditatively.

If you are married and read a newspaper article aloud to your spouse, you don't do it mindlessly. You wish to convey meaning to the person you love. Your heart and mind listen and observe as you read. Even though you read the words of someone else, you enter into the purpose and sentiment of those words and they become your own. They are a vehicle for expressing your thoughts, hopes, and longings to the other.

Our use of formal prayers should work the same way. As we bring those words to God, we also bring the meaning that they convey. We pray them in the presence of God, Who can work in our hearts and minds through His Holy Spirit to form us and mold us into strong, faithful Christians. God will help us to take the thoughts and sentiments of our formal prayers as our very own. Over time, we will experience His love for us as we pray in this manner.

As valuable as formal prayers can be, we should still reserve a generous part of our prayer time for conversation with God. Christ is present, and you have made an act of the will to be present with Him. He loves you more than anyone in this world loves you. He desires to hear you and speak with you. Our Lord is concerned with every aspect of your life. You can speak to Jesus about any and every element of your life. Tell Him of your needs, fears, frustrations, angers, sorrows, and hopes. Speak words of love, praise, and thanksgiving. You don't need to speak any special language to Him. He knows you. Just tell Him what's on your mind, in the words you would use with your best friend.

Sometimes, we can experience great consolations in prayer. At other times we may feel dry and alone. The secret is to be consistent. When you don't know how or what to pray, there are several practical steps you can take. First, tell God of your difficulty and ask for His grace. Secondly, you can use some spiritual book to help you begin to talk to God. The Holy Scriptures are unsurpassed as tools for prayer. You can begin by asking the Holy Spirit, Who inspired the writer, to inspire you, the reader. Read a small passage of the Scripture and consider what it says to you personally. Then use it as a place to jump into prayer. Talk directly to God about what that passage is saying to you.

If the passage is extolling God for His greatness, then tell Him how much He means in your own life, or how much you would like Him to mean. Ask Him to make you as devoted as the writer you just read. If the passage speaks of our responsibilities as Christians, take the opportunity to review how well you are carrying out your duties. Ask God's forgiveness where you have failed and ask His grace so that you may improve. Ask Him to show you specific areas where you might improve.

End your prayer at the time you've predetermined. If you had set aside fifteen minutes for prayer, end after fifteen minutes. Finish by thanking God for the opportunity to spend time with Him and tell Him you desire to follow Him faithfully. Always keep in mind that you can say these things even if you don't particularly "feel" them at the moment. Presumably, you would like to feel them. Show the beginnings of faith by speaking as you will when God gives you greater grace, as He surely will. The great philosopher Blaise Pascal advised that we are cured of our lukewarmness by carrying out the actions "that will make you believe quite naturally, and will make you more docile." It's good to end your prayer with the Sign of the Cross.

Many people find it helpful to jot down some thought or sentiment from their prayer. Later in the day you can refer to this note and allow it to encourage you that God is always near and working in and through you.

Hold That Thought

Mother Teresa of Calcutta said that God does not require us to be successful but rather faithful. This can apply to prayer. Prayer is an Act of Love of God, and true love does not depend upon the excitement of our feelings. If we approach prayer primarily as our opportunity to show our love for God, we will be less concerned about how well we feel at a given moment. A parent is pleased with the child's efforts to communicate, even if the words are unintelligible. In the same way, God is pleased with our efforts and our commitment to pray. Even though we should not focus on what we can "get" out of prayer, we can take great comfort in the fact that God is faithful in His love for us. As we come to Him in prayer, He will work in our hearts and minds. Often the changes in us are gradual and we may not be able to immediately perceive them. Yet, when we view our lives over time, we will see the changes that God has effected through faithfulness in prayer.

Say Your Prayers

"Mental prayer is nothing but a friendly conversation in which the soul speaks, heart to heart, with the One Who we know loves us."

— St. Teresa of Ávila

"Prayer is not a number of reflections and resolutions; it is personal, intimate, loving contact and [conversation] with a friend who is loved and by whom the soul understands that it itself is loved."

— Robert Nash, S.J.

"[Prayer] is commonly held to be a conversation. In a conversation there are always an 'I' and a 'thou' or 'you.' In this case the 'Thou' is with a capital 'T.' If at the first the 'I' seems to be the most important element in prayer, prayer teaches that the situation is different. The 'Thou' is more important, because our prayer begins with God."

— Pope John Paul II

"In the New Covenant, prayer is the living relationship of the children of God with their Father Who is good beyond measure, with His Son Jesus Christ and with the Holy Spirit."

— Catechism of the Catholic Church (CCC), no. 2565

Catholic Prayers

How to Pray
the Sign of the Cross

There are three common ways of making the Sign of the Cross. The most prevalent one in personal devotion is known as the "large cross." We begin by touching the forehead with the tip of the right hand. Then proceed to the middle of the chest and finally both shoulders, first the left and then the right. While making the Sign of the Cross we say: "In the name of the Father and of the Son and of the Holy Spirit."

The second form is called the "small cross." This is the most ancient form of the gesture. Here the thumb is used to trace a cross on the forehead. Today, this form is used in both Baptism and Confirmation. In Baptism, the minister, parents, and godparents all trace the Sign of the Cross on the child. In Confirmation, the bishop or priest traces the cross with the oil of chrism on the forehead of the recipient.

The third form is used in extending a blessing. In this formula the priest or minister traces the Sign of the Cross in the air and prays over the person or object that is being blessed.

In current practice in the Western Church, the right hand is slightly cupped as the Sign of the Cross is made — though there are variations. In the fifth century, the Church was plagued by a heresy that claimed Christ had only one nature. Partly in reaction to this heresy, people began to make the large cross by using two fingers. This was a sign of their belief in the two natures of Christ. Sometime later, in the East, people began to use the thumb, index, and middle finger, pressed together at the fingertips, to make the hand movement. Those three fingers together symbolized the Trinity and Unity of God, while the two fingers folded against the palm of the hand symbolized the two

"Holy God, Holy Strong One, Holy Immortal One, Have mercy on us."

— **Common Invocation of the Eastern Churches**

natures of Jesus Christ, both divine and human. This practice is still prevalent in the Eastern Churches.

You may on occasion see someone kiss his or her fingers after completing the Sign of the Cross. This is common in Hispanic cultures. If you look closely, you'll notice that person is making a second Sign of the Cross by placing the thumb across the index finger. The kiss that ends the gesture is a sign of devotion to the cross.

The cross has been the symbol of Christians from the first centuries. As St. Paul says in his letter to Galatians: "May I never boast except in the cross of Our Lord Jesus Christ, through which the world has been crucified to me, and I to the world" (Gal 6:14 NAB). The making of the Sign of the Cross on one's person proclaimed belief in the faith.

In the Book of Revelation (Rev 7:3 and 9:4) the sacred author states that the faithful will be recognized by the "seal of God on their foreheads." Some commentators have identified this with the Sign of the Cross. In earlier ages, this scriptural connection was more explicit, as the gesture was called the "sign of Christ" and the "seal of the living God."

Hold That Thought

Sometimes, baseball players make the Sign of the Cross before stepping up to bat. Is this superstition, habit, devotion, or a silent prayer? Depending on the attitude of the person, it can be any of these.

The Sign of the Cross can remind us who we are. Christ has redeemed us through the cross. His sacrifice has given us new life. That fact influences our approach to all aspects of life, from waking up to playing sports. So, to make a Sign of the Cross before beginning our prayer, work, or any aspect of our daily activity gives us perspective. It can draw our thoughts to center on the person we have become in Christ and the relationship that we have with God.

Spiritual writers speak of the Sign of the Cross as a source of strength in times of temptation and difficulties. This is not to be taken in a superstitious way. Rather, the act is both a silent prayer by which we place ourselves under the protection of the triumphant cross of Christ.

Many people "bracket" their prayers with the Sign of the Cross. We begin to pray by this gesture that acknowledges that we belong to Christ and that we come into God's presence through the redemptive grace of the cross. The same sign ends our prayers as we put on the shield of faith to go forth to live the Christian life in the world.

"Bless yourself with the Sign of the Cross, to chase away the fiend with all his devils. For, as Chrysostom says, whenever the devil sees the sign of the holy cross, he dreads it as the staff with which he is beaten. And in this blessing you begin with your hand at the head downward, and then to the left side and believe that our Lord Jesus Christ came down from the head, that is from the Father into earth by His holy incarnation, and from earth into the left side, that is hell, by His bitter Passion, and from thence into His Father's right side by His glorious Ascension."

— **12th-century instructions to Bridgettine Nuns of Sion**

The Sign of the Cross

"In all our travels, in our coming and going out, in putting on our clothes and our shoes, at table, in going to rest, whatever employment occupies us, we mark our forehead with the Sign of the Cross."

— Tertullian

"My son, mark all your actions with the sign of the life-giving cross. Do not go out from the door of your house till you have signed yourself with the cross. Do not neglect that sign whether in eating or drinking or going to sleep, or in the home or going on a journey. There is no habit to be compared with it. Let it be a protecting wall round all your conduct, and teach it to your children that they may earnestly learn the custom."

— St. Ephrem of Syria

"Blessed is our God at all times, now and always and forever. Amen."

— Byzantine invocation used when making the Sign of the Cross

How to Pray
the Basic Prayers:
Our Father,
Hail Mary, Glory Be

Memorized formal prayers can play an important part in your spiritual life. Three prayers especially have been held in high esteem through Christian history, and so they merit our special attention as we begin to pray. We must remember that prayer is a "raising of the mind and heart to God." Specific words, therefore, have a secondary place. The simple pronunciation of the name "Jesus," when said with meaning and devotion, can be more prayerful than the recitation of a book of prayers, if they are said with lack of recollection and intention.

Still, forms can be quite useful. When the heart or mind desires to call out to God, whether in joy or sorrow, in petition or in difficulty, we'll often find it helpful to join our thoughts and affections to words. Here, memorized prayers, especially the three we are considering, can come in handy.

Moreover, repeating these prayers does not diminish their value. No one ever tires of hearing a loved one say: "I love you." Any prayer said with devotion is pleasing to God.

The Our Father, Hail Mary, and Glory Be are often the first catechism for children. From these prayers, Catholics young and old learn basic elements of our faith and learn how to honor God. Yet there is a depth to these prayers that can continue to teach and encourage us, no matter our age or stage of spiritual development. These are prayers we never outgrow.

The Our Father

This is the prayer that Our Lord taught to His disciples when they asked Him to teach them how to pray (see Mt 6:9-11 and Lk 11:2-4). It is sometimes called the perfect prayer, because it contains so much in so few words: adoration, praise, petition, contrition. One early Christian, named Tertullian, identified the Lord's Prayer as the "summary of the whole Gospel." The *Catechism of the Catholic Church* presents a long exposition on this prayer (nos. 2761-2865). All of our prayer can be considered an outgrowth of this single prayer:

Our Father, Who art in heaven,
hallowed be Thy name.
Thy kingdom come;
Thy will be done on earth as it is in heaven.
Give us this day our daily bread;
and forgive us our trespasses as we forgive
those who trespass against us;
and lead us not into temptation,
but deliver us from evil.
Amen.

As we begin to pray the Lord's Prayer, we should pause to consider that we are children speaking to a perfect Father — a Father Who always provides, a Father Who never ceases to love, a Father always ready and willing to teach and to help. In our hearts, we should consciously "look" toward the Father as we pray; for we are not just speaking words to the wind, but to a Person.

The prayer begins, then, with the petitions for the glory of God, the coming of His kingdom and the fulfillment of His will. We can add our own praise and adoration as we speak these words. The next four petitions present our desires to God. We ask Him to provide for our needs. We

24

ask for healing and forgiveness of our sins and for victory in our struggle against evil.

At the end of the prayer, many early Christians added the phrase: "for Thine is the kingdom and the power and the glory forever." The prayer concludes with "Amen," which means "So be it," words that emphasize our acceptance of the all the petitions of the Lord's Prayer.

Our Father, Who Art . . .

"Faith, hope, and charity lead unto God the man who prays, that is, the man who believes, who hopes, who desires, and he is guided as to what he should ask of the Lord by studying the Lord's Prayer."

— **St. Augustine**

"The Lord's Prayer is the most perfect of prayers . . . In it we ask, not only for all the things we can rightly desire, but also in the sequence that they should be desired. This prayer not only teaches us to ask for things, but also in what order we should desire them."

— **St. Thomas Aquinas**

The Hail Mary

This is another prayer that is both scriptural and theologically significant:

**Hail Mary, full of grace, the Lord is with thee;
blessed art thou among women,
and blessed is the fruit of thy womb, Jesus.
Holy Mary, Mother of God,
pray for us sinners,
now and at the hour of our death.
Amen.**

The first sentence of the prayer is the greeting of the angel Gabriel to Mary at the Annunciation (Lk 1:28). By joining our voices with that of the angel, we acknowledge God's saving plan, give glory to Jesus, the God-man, pay honor to Mary who is mother of Jesus, and, by extension, is also our mother and the mother of the Church. Remember, after all, that Jesus, while dying on the cross, gave Mary to be a mother to His beloved disciple (Jn 19:26-27). We are all Jesus' beloved disciples now, and so she is mother to us all.

As we pray the Hail Mary, we should look to this loving mother. Sometimes it helps if we pray before an image of her. We can silently recall Mary's response to the message of the Annunciation: "Let it be done to me according to your word." This can be our prayer along with her. As she accepted God's will in her life, we pray with her and to her for the grace to yield willingly to God's plan for our lives.

In the second half of the prayer, we place ourselves in the loving hands of our mother and ask for her intercession that we may triumph over sin and remain faithful to God, so that one day we may join her before the throne of the risen Christ.

Full of Grace

"By asking Mary to pray for us, we acknowledge ourselves to be poor sinners and we address ourselves to the 'Mother of Mercy,' the All-Holy One. We give ourselves over to her now, in the Today of our lives. And our trust broadens further, already at the present moment, to surrender 'the hour of our death' wholly to her care. May she be there as she was at her son's death on the cross. May she welcome us as our mother at the hour of our passing to lead us to her son, Jesus, in paradise."

— CCC, no. 2677

"By each Hail Mary we give our Lady the same honor that God gave her when He sent the angel Gabriel to greet her for Him."

**— From *The Secret of the Rosary*,
St. Louis de Montfort**

The Glory Be

So many of our prayers contain petitions and requests. The Glory Be is a short prayer in which we seek only to give glory to God as we proclaim the great mystery of the Trinity:

Glory be to the Father, and to the Son, and to
the Holy Spirit.
As it was in the beginning, is now,
and ever shall be, world without end.
Amen.

"The faith of all Christians rests on the Trinity."

— St. Caesarius of Arles

The simple prayer proclaims that God is one, and yet God is three Persons: Father, Son, and Holy Spirit. This is the most foundational truth of the Christian faith. The phrase "world without end" is an old-fashioned way of saying "forever." Our God, one in three, is eternal and unchanging.

Father, Son, and Holy Spirit

"The mystery of the Most Holy Trinity is the central mystery of Christian faith and life. It is the mystery of God in Himself. It is therefore the source of all the other mysteries of faith, the light that enlightens them."

— CCC, no. 234

How to Make a Morning Offering

The *Catechism of the Catholic Church* tells us, "The Tradition of the Church proposes to the faithful certain rhythms of praying intended to nourish continual prayer. Some are daily, such as morning and evening. . . . [These] are also basic rhythms of the Christian's life of prayer" (no. 2698). As they rise from bed, many people will make the Sign of the Cross and recite a prayer that gives the day to Our Lord. This action testifies to the fact we are the Lord's and that we begin everything in and through Him.

In 1844, Jesuit Father Francois Xavier Gaulrelet penned a prayer that is still used to this day. The prayer is the Morning Offering to the Sacred Heart of Jesus:

O Jesus, through the Immaculate Heart of Mary, I offer You my prayers, works, joys, and sufferings of this day for all the intentions of Your Sacred Heart, in union with the Holy Sacrifice of the Mass throughout the world, in reparation for my sins, for the intentions of all our associates, and in particular for the intentions of our Holy Father this month.

The tradition of offering our day to God is an ancient practice, but Father Gaulrelet's prayer formalized that intention in a memorable (and easily memorized) way. Through this prayer, we join our plea to the Eucharistic prayer of each Mass. The Mass is the liturgical re-presentation of the loving sacrifice of Jesus on Calvary. We, by the Morning Offering, unite our thoughts and actions to that one eternal sacrifice. This union grants rich meaning and value to every aspect of our day. In the Morning Offering, we also ask the intercession of our mother, Mary, as we pray through her "Immaculate Heart." Our prayers are united with those of millions of Catholics all over the world who offer the same intention of prayer every morning.

Pope John Paul II said that the Morning Offering is "of fundamental importance in the life of each and every one of the faithful." In the box on the next page is a quote from Jesuit Father Walter Ciszek, who for years was jailed in communist prison camps. He had very little control over the outer aspects of his life. His daily sufferings often included torture and deprivation of food and water. Yet, he lived by his Morning Offering and accepted everything from God's hand, and he offered it all together with the suffering of Jesus. Communism has come and gone in Russia, but surely the holy offering of Father Ciszek still brings grace to the land.

Hold That Thought

The Morning Offering includes the intentions of our bishops and especially the intentions of the Holy Father as part of the prayer. The burdens carried by the Holy Father and the bishops are great. The faithful have an obligation to pray for them regularly. A good practice is to pray, each morning, specifically for the Pope and the bishop of your diocese. Many people say an Our Father, Hail Mary, and Glory Be with the specific intention of the needs of the Pope, and then pray another set specifically for their bishop.

Morning prayers can also be offered privately while preparing for the day (while shaving, bathing, fixing hair, and so on). Yet there is great advantage to saying at least some morning prayer, perhaps the Morning Offering, as a family. It sets the tone not only for the individual, but also for the family. By so doing, we unite our corporate family life under the Lordship and merciful heart of Christ.

Get a Good Start

"The simple soul who each day makes a Morning Offering of all the prayers, works, joys, and sufferings of this day — and who then acts upon it by accepting unquestioningly and responding lovingly to all the situations of the day as truly sent by God has perceived with an almost childlike faith the profound truth about the will of God. The plain and simple truth is that His will is what He actually wills to send us each day, in the way of circumstances, places, people, and problems. The trick is to see that . . . every day."

— From *He Leadeth Me*,
Father Walter J. Ciszek, S.J.

"[T]heir work, prayers, and apostolic endeavors, their ordinary married and family life, their daily labor, their mental and physical relaxation . . . all these become spiritual sacrifices acceptable to God through Jesus Christ. During the celebration of the Eucharist these sacrifices are most lovingly offered to the Father along with the Lord's body. Thus as worshipers whose deed is holy, the lay faithful consecrate the world itself to God."

— *Lumen Gentium*, no. 34

"Most Holy and Adorable Trinity, one God in three Persons, I praise You and give You thanks for all the favors You have bestowed on me. Your goodness has preserved me until now. I offer You my whole being and in particular all my thoughts, words, and deeds, together with all the trials I may undergo today. Give them Your blessing. May Your divine Love animate them and may they serve Your greater glory. I make this Morning Offering in union with the divine intentions of Jesus Christ Who offers Himself daily in the Sacrifice of the Mass and in union with Mary, His Virgin Mother and our Mother, who was always the faithful handmaid of the Lord."

— Morning Offering

How to Pray at Mealtimes

There is something special about sharing a meal. It is often a moment of peace in a hectic day, drawing together those who share in it.

Whenever we eat, whether alone or together, we want to acknowledge that God is present and ask Him to bless our food and those who partake of it. After everyone is comfortably settled at table, the prayer begins with the Sign of the Cross. The traditional mealtime prayer, often called "Grace," is:

> **Bless us, O Lord, and these Your gifts,**
> **which we are about to receive from**
> **Your bounty,**
> **through Christ Our Lord. Amen.**

A Sign of the Cross normally ends the prayer.

One added value to this practice is that it helps us acknowledge God's presence in all the aspects of our daily lives. It creates a sense of thankfulness and of the presence of God. The Scripture directs us: "Whether you eat or drink, or whatever you do, do everything for the glory of God" (1 Cor 10:31 NAB).

Food nourishes our bodies, and it also reminds us that Jesus nourishes us spiritually through the gift of Himself in the Eucharist. He chose to make a family meal the central sacrament, the source and summit, of the Christian faith. Our moment of prayer at mealtime is an acknowledgement that, as our ordinary meal will eliminate our bodily hunger, we long for Jesus to fill our spiritual hunger through the Eucharist.

Consider This

The blessing before meals is a great teaching opportunity with children. They will learn both the prayer and the Sign of the Cross. They will also learn that faith in God is an important part of family identity. It is important to be consistent so that children realize: "As a Catholic family we begin our meals with prayer." Thus, your meals should begin with Grace when your gathering includes only the family, but also when you have company for dinner or when you're eating at a restaurant.

Blessings at Meals

Lord Jesus Christ, may our Lenten fasting turn us toward all our brothers and sisters who are in need. Bless this table, our good food, and ourselves. Send us through Lent with good cheer, and bring us to the fullness of Your passover.

— Meal Prayer for Lent, From *Catholic Household Blessings & Prayers*

We joyfully sing Your praises, Lord Jesus Christ, Who on the day of Your resurrection was recognized by Your disciples in the breaking of the bread. Remain here with us as we gratefully partake of the gifts and at the banquet table in heaven welcome us, who have welcomed You in our brothers and sisters, for You live and reign for ever and ever. Amen.

— Meal Prayer for Easter, From *Catholic Household Blessings & Prayers*

How to Make an Act of Faith

Objectively, the word *faith* refers to the truths revealed by God in the Scriptures and through Tradition as preserved and handed on by the Church. That's what we mean when we speak of "the Catholic faith." Subjectively, *faith* is one of the three theological virtues, which also include hope and love. Faith, in this sense, is the virtue by which we accept what has been revealed by God. That's what it means to say "I have faith."

To make an Act of Faith, then, is to recite a prayer that expresses your personal acceptance of all that the Lord has revealed to be true. This is something we all should do often, perhaps weekly or even daily if we feel the need. The Traditional Act of Faith is:

O my God!
I firmly believe that You are one God in three
divine persons, Father, Son, and Holy Spirit;
I believe that Your divine Son became man
and died for our sins,
and that He will come to judge
the living and the dead.
I believe these and all the truths which
the Holy Catholic Church teaches,
because You have revealed them,
Who can neither deceive nor be deceived.

Faith is primarily a divine gift. When Peter made his profession of faith that Jesus is the Christ (Mt 16:16-17), Jesus said: "Flesh and blood has not revealed this to you, but My Father Who is in heaven." Apart from the action of God, faith is impossible for man. However, the Holy Spirit supernaturally bestows the gift of faith upon men.

35

"Faith is to believe what you do not see; the reward of this faith is to see what you believe."

— **St. Augustine**

_____

The Holy Spirit not only gives the gift; He also works in our will through grace so that we may respond.

This points to the other aspect of faith: God gives the gift, but we must reply. It is as if a friend gave you a new article of clothing. It does you no good unless you accept it and wear it. The gift of faith is free; we only need to put it on — and the Holy Spirit even helps us to get dressed!

The *Catechism of the Catholic Church* goes right to the point: "Believing is possible only by grace and the interior helps of the Holy Spirit. But it is no less true that believing is an authentic human act . . . In faith, the human intellect and will cooperate with divine grace" (nos. 154-155). The Act of Faith, then, is a personal act by which we freely respond to the initiative of God.

Yet if we have made an initial profession of faith, why do we need to continue reciting creeds and praying the formal prayer called the Act of Faith? One reason is that our personal "yes" to God — our acceptance of His gift — is not merely a one-time event. Responding to faith is a constant, daily part of our Christian life. As we continue to actively receive the gift, God continues to give the gift to us. Our spiritual wardrobe gets filled with faith gifts as we continue to respond.

Also, faith needs to grow in understanding. St. Augustine wrote that "understanding is the reward of faith." As we make statements of faith in prayer, and by reciting the creed, and as we meditate upon these truths, our intellect will come to embrace the truth more fully. We must remember, after all, that our faith is not primarily in statements and decrees, but in God. We believe in the Fatherhood of God not as something dry and sterile, but rather as a lived reality that makes a profound difference in our lives. Belief that God is our Father changes our view of ourselves and of others. It affects how we relate to others and how we deal with difficulties. To pray and meditate about our faith allows us to grow in our understanding of the truth and in our love with the giver of truth.

Hold That Thought

Most people will endure times when they struggle with faith. That is not unusual. Yet our struggles can lead us closer to God if we step up to Him from the foundation of the faith He has given us. The Gospel gives us a good illustration of this principle in the story of a man whose son was possessed by the devil (Mk 9:14-29). The man brought the boy to the disciples of Jesus with the request that they heal the boy, but the disciples were unable to do so. By the time Jesus joined the group, the father seems to have been struggling with faith that Jesus could actually heal the boy. He even qualifies his request: *"If you can do anything . . .* help us." Jesus responded by telling the father: "All things are possible for him who believes." The father then responds with both a statement of faith and a prayer for the strengthening of that faith: "Lord, I believe, help my unbelief!"

We can follow the same pattern. When we struggle with some issue of faith, we can begin with a statement of faith. "Lord, I believe in You, in Your word, in Your church, and in Your love for me." We then can ask for God's grace in our struggles. "Lord, help my unbelief!"

Lord, I Believe in You

"But you, beloved, who possess this faith, or who have begun now newly to have it, let it be nourished and increase in you. For as things temporal have come, so long before foretold, so will things eternal also come, which are promised."

— St. Augustine

"The integral Christian is the man who not only submits his judgements to the truths of the faith, but strives, in addition, to have his whole life guided by the spirit of faith. . . . We are Christians to the exact degree in which 'faith' is the controlling motive in our thoughts, views, decisions, and actions."

— Edward Leen

"If we Christians really lived in accordance with our faith, the greatest revolution of all times would take place. The effectiveness of our co-redemption depends on each one of us. You should mediate on this."

— Blessed Josémaria Escrivá

How to Make an Act of Hope

"I sure hope I win the lottery!" Well, hitting the jackpot may or may not be a good thing. And that statement is at best wishful thinking. It certainly has nothing to do with the theological virtue of hope.

The virtue of hope is given to us at Baptism. Unlike the lottery, it is a sure bet. Hope is based on certainty because it is founded on Christ and on His promises. Do you want eternal life? No problem; Christ has overcome sin and death and provides a channel for relationship with the Father. Do you want truth? Christ has revealed the mind and heart of God. He has given the Holy Spirit to guide you in the ways of truth. Maybe you'd like to hit the jackpot and find both meaning and love. Well, as a baptized Christian, you hold the winning ticket. Christ has loved you first and granted you His sanctifying grace. You are on a path that leads to the ultimate prize: life eternal in Christ.

To make an Act of Hope, then, is to set your sight firmly on the goal, knowing in your heart that God will take you there, and asking Him to speed you along the way. Praying these prayers can help you to gain endurance, optimism, and strength to go on. The traditional Act of Hope is:

O my God, relying on Your almighty power and infinite mercy and promises, I hope to obtain pardon for my sins, the help of Your grace, and life everlasting, through the merits of Jesus Christ, my Lord and Redeemer.

You may want to say at this point: "If God freely gives me everything, what is hope about?" The lottery comparison can still help. You might have the winning ticket, but even that is useless if you neglect to cash it in. And if you lose that ticket — through your own carelessness — you forfeit the prize.

Our hope is sure because Jesus is fully trustworthy. Still, you and I are the other side of the hope equation. Through carelessness or bad will, we can fail to respond to God. We can reject the mercy of God and live only for ourselves. We can even be tempted to the sin of despair, totally rejecting hope in God's love and power to save us. Then we've lost our ticket.

The virtue of hope is given freely to us at Baptism. But we cannot let it lie dormant. We must consciously live this virtue by actively placing our trust in God. Continual acts of trust strengthen our inner conviction that God loves us and provides for us. This conviction then leads us to rely more on God's promise. Thus, hope is a virtue that can continue to put down deeper roots and bloom more beautiful flowers in our lives. To use another analogy: a muscle never used is still a muscle, but a muscle that is exercised has real power to work. Hope grows and becomes a greater influence in our lives as we exercise our trust in God — as we make Acts of Hope a vital part of our prayer.

Christian hope is the basis of joy and realistic optimism. Even when we are in difficult situations, hope assures us that we rest in God's hands. We find solace knowing that He loves us and allows even suffering for our good. Christian hope gives us a perspective that goes beyond our immediate circumstances and allows us to see the horizon.

"My whole hope is nowhere but in Your exceeding great mercy."

— **St. Augustine**

40

Consider This

"Through [Jesus Christ] we have obtained access to this grace in which we stand, and we rejoice in our hope of sharing the glory of God. More than that, we rejoice in our sufferings, knowing that suffering produces endurance, and endurance produces character, and character produces hope, and hope does not disappoint us, because God's love has been poured into our hearts through the Holy Spirit which has been given to us" (Rom 5:2-5).

Here St. Paul shows us how hope develops in our lives. We start from a basis of hope founded in grace and we anticipate "sharing in the glory of God." When suffering comes into our lives, Paul tells us to "rejoice" in the suffering. It's not that suffering is pleasant, but that suffering accepted with hope and trust can lead us somewhere — to a share in the glory of God. Suffering can also foster our strength and endurance. Endurance, in turn, allows us to better handle other difficulties that come our way. Over time, that virtue becomes so rooted in our lives that it becomes a character trait that allows us to see life from the perspective of eternity. That's hope.

If we struggle with a negative attitude and are prone to lack trust, there are many helps available to us. For example, we can read the lives of the saints. Many of them went through trials but, through all, they hoped and trusted in God. Their example can motivate us to greater trust. Whenever we find ourselves slipping into negativity, we can also consciously make an Act of Hope, in our own words or in the words of the traditional prayer. When we actively speak words of trust and hope, our feelings are more likely to "catch up.

Our Hope Is Sure

"[Christ] has now reconciled [you] in His body of flesh by His death, in order to present you holy and blameless and irreproachable before Him, provided that you continue in the faith, stable and steadfast, not shifting from the hope of the Gospel which you heard."

— Colossians 1:22-23

"When the goodness and loving kindness of God our Savior appeared, He saved us, not because of deeds done by us in righteousness, but in virtue of His own mercy, by the washing of regeneration and renewal in the Holy Spirit, which He poured out upon us richly through Jesus Christ our Savior, so that we might be justified by His grace and become heirs in hope of eternal life."

— Titus 3: 4-7

"It is impossible that God should prove false. We who have fled for refuge might have strong encouragement to seize the hope set before us."

— Hebrews 6:18

How to Make
an Act of Charity (Love)

Charity, or love, is the most important gift God gives us at Baptism. Without divine love, which is His very life, we could never love as God requires us to love. For we must love perfectly, as He does.

Still, we have the responsibility to exercise the gift of divine love, through our life and our works, but also through prayers that explicitly express our love. Tradition calls these prayers "Acts of Charity" or "Acts of Love." The most popular form of this prayer is:

O my God, I love You above all things, with my whole heart and soul, because You are all-good and worthy of all love. I love my neighbor as myself for the love of You. I forgive all who have injured me and ask pardon of all whom I have injured.

The first object of our love must be God Himself. We are called to love God above everything else — with our whole heart, mind, and soul. Love of God is called the queen of all virtues. All other virtues lead us toward God; only love unites us to God. And from divine love springs all other virtues.

How do we love God? First, by avoiding sin. When we love someone, we avoid doing things that displease our beloved. But, more than that, we strive to do things that please that person. Thus we should also show our love for God by keeping His commandments and doing good works.

Yet love of God is not all that is required of us. We must also love our neighbor, meaning everyone we meet

"Love, and love alone, is the heritage and heart, motive and mainspring in the life of the Church."

— **St. Francis de Sales**

— not only those who love us and do good to us. God asks us to love as He loves, and His love reaches out to everyone (see the *Catechism of the Catholic Church*, no. 1825). Thus we love our neighbor not because she is a likable person, because she is similar to us, or because we get along well with her. We love our neighbor because God loves our neighbor and calls us to do the same.

We are to be a channel, an instrument, of God's love to every neighbor. If we love others with the love of God, we bless them with a supernatural love. The Holy Spirit can work through us to embrace them with the love of God.

Isn't it impossible to love everybody? Yes, it's impossible for human beings, but all things are possible with God. Living divine love, activating the gift of Baptism, requires effort on our part. Sometimes it's not easy to love with God's love; we have to work at it. After all, some of those people included in "everybody" are people we don't particularly like — and perhaps even people whom we want to hate.

How do we love someone who has injured a member of our family? How do we love those who wish evil upon us? We do it only by God's grace. Divine love does not rely upon our emotions. It involves an act of our will. We have to say: "Out of love of God, I choose to love this person." That's one kind of Act of Love.

Sometimes on the news we see victims of crime who have forgiven the criminals who caused them to suffer — wounded them, stole from them, slandered them, defrauded them. Nonbelievers cannot comprehend how such forgiveness is possible. The "natural" human instinct seems to be revenge. Yet that is why Christian love is so powerful — it seems so radically opposed to our angry instincts that it must have its roots in God. Throughout history, unconditional Christian love has inspired the conversion of many, including one-time murderers, persecutors, and torturers.

We normally don't wake up one day and perform some extraordinary Act of Love and sacrifice. We grow in love. Small acts of love open us to God's grace and to greater Acts of Love. A smile, a helping hand, an encouraging word — all these activate God's love in us. All these are Acts of Love.

If imitation is the greatest form of praise, then we truly praise God when we love as He would love. Jesus died for sinners — those who rejected Him. We lay down our lives so that the love of God may reach our neighbor.

"He who abides in Love, abides in God, and God in him."

—1 John 4:16

Consider This

Sometimes it's prudent to abandon the use of an older term for a newer one that's more understandable to a new generation. For example, few people today use "thee" and "thy" in everyday speech. So many people substitute "you" and "your" in their prayers. But sometimes there is value in retaining an older word. There is a good argument for maintaining the traditional word "charity" rather than the readily recognized word "love." Ask someone the meaning of love and his or her working definition probably won't mention God. Even the dictionary definition falls far short of the Christian meaning. The *American Heritage Dictionary* defines love as "(a) a . . . feeling of affection, (b) intense desire and attraction toward a person, the emotion of sex and romance, (c) sexual passion," and so on. None of these comes close to Christian love.

So perhaps "charity" still serves us best. At least its dictionary entry includes: "The virtue defined as love directed first toward God but also toward oneself and one's neighbors as objects of God's love."

"Love your enemies, do good to those who hate you, bless those who curse you, pray for those who mistreat you."

— Luke 6:27-28 (NAB)

Abide in Love

"Acts of Love . . . are the fuel with which the fire of divine love is kept burning in our hearts."

— **St. Alphonsus Liguori**

"Whoever says, 'I love God,' but hates his brother, is a liar; for whoever does not love a brother, whom he has seen, cannot love God, Whom he has not seen."

— **1 John 4:20**

"[Love] is the mother, the root, the fountainhead whence the other virtues have their origin; inasmuch as it stamps them all with that divine character which renders them worthy of an everlasting reward."

— **St. Thomas Aquinas**

"Love consists not in the extent of our happiness, but in the firmness of our determination to try to please God in everything, and to endeavor in all possible ways not to offend Him, and to pray Him ever to advance the honor and glory of His Son and the growth of the Catholic Church."

— **St. Teresa of Ávila**

"Man's love for God owes its origin, growth, and perfection to God's eternal love for man. . . . Everything we have is God's gift to us — above all, the supernatural blessings of charity. If they are ours by gift, why boast about them?"

— **St. Francis de Sales**

[Our Lord said to His Disciples,] "A new Commandment I give you: that you love one another as I have loved you."

— John 13:34

"Be as God to the unfortunate, by imitating the mercy of God. For in nothing do we draw so close to God as in doing good to God."

— St. Gregory Nazianzen

"No one should think that he observes this law [of charity] because he loves his neighbor. For he who loves others, but not for God's sake, has not charity, even though he may think he has. True charity lies in loving our friend with and in God, and our enemy for God's sake. He loves for God's sake Who loves even those by whom he is not loved."

— Pope St. Gregory the Great

"Love is itself the fulfillment of all our works. There is the goal; that is why we run: we run toward it, and once we reach it, in it we shall find rest."

— St. Augustine

How to Pray the Jesus Prayer

St. Paul tells us "to pray without ceasing" (1 Thess 5:17; Col 4:2) and to "be constant in prayer" (Rom 12:12). The Jesus Prayer is an ancient practice that aims to make prayer as regular and as constant as our breathing.

**Lord Jesus Christ,
Son of the living God,
have mercy on me, a sinner!**

This is the Jesus Prayer. It is intentionally short, so that it can be uttered in one breath, and can be uttered continuously, once with each breath. Its regular recitation ushers us into God's presence.

A longstanding tradition in the Eastern Churches, the Jesus Prayer is also called "the prayer of the heart." It provides a means of concentration, a point of focus for the inner life. Although the prayer is short, it is packed with meaning. It acknowledges Jesus as Lord, Savior, Messiah, God, and Son of the Father. It acknowledges that we stand as sinners before God, and that we seek His mercy.

A related Eastern tradition is the prayer of the name of Jesus. In biblical times, a person's name had a sacred character. Note how often God changed people's names based on the relationship they had with Him. Abram became Abraham; Jacob received the name Israel; and Saul, in the New Testament, became Paul.

God's name was particularly sacred. God revealed Himself to Moses as "I am." As the names of the patriarchs revealed God's relationship to them, so God's name showed both His own nature and His relationship to the Israelites. "I am" was the one Who lived eternally, and "I am" was the one relating to Moses and His people. God's

49

> "Whatever you ask in My name, I will do it, that the Father may be glorified in the Son; if you ask anything in My name, I will do it."
>
> — John 14:13-14

---

name was so revered that the devout Jew would neither write the name nor say it.

In the New Testament, the name of Jesus was identified with His person and His power. Devils are cast out by the "name" of Jesus (Lk 10:17) and cures are worked by the power of the "name" (Acts 3). Christians were people of the "name" — followers of Jesus. To invoke the name of Jesus was possible because of the relationship between Christ and His disciples. In saying "Jesus," the disciple tapped into all that the name meant — Savior, King, Lord, Provider, and so on.

The Jesus Prayer focuses on the name of Jesus. Thus the devout recitation of the prayer touches the depth of the relationship and power of the person behind that name, Jesus.

The Jesus Prayer is normally said slowly and in rhythm with one's breathing. The person focuses on Jesus Christ while the words provide an entrance to prayer.

Hold That Thought

The Jesus Prayer is helpful always, but especially when there is tension and anxiety in life. The method itself has a natural calming effect. The Savior's name brings comfort when, perhaps, it is difficult for us to find words. At the same time, Jesus hears our prayers and brings the supernatural peace that surpasses understanding.

Have Mercy on Me

"Therefore God has highly exalted Him and bestowed on Him the name which is above every name, that at the name of Jesus every knee should bow, in heaven and on earth and under the earth, and every tongue confess that Jesus Christ is Lord, to the glory of God the Father."

— **Philippians 2:9-11**

"And a man lame from birth was being carried, whom they laid daily at that gate of the temple which is called Beautiful to ask alms of those who entered the temple. Seeing Peter and John about to go into the temple, he asked for alms. And Peter directed his gaze at him, with John, and said, 'Look at us.' And he fixed his attention upon them, expecting to receive something from them. But Peter said, 'I have no silver and gold, but I give you what I have; in the name of Jesus Christ of Nazareth, walk.' And He took him by the right hand and raised him up; and immediately his feet and ankles were made strong."

— **Acts 3:2-7**

"But the tax collector, standing far off, would not even lift up his eyes to heaven, but beat his breast, saying, 'God, be merciful to me a sinner!' "

— **Luke 18:13**

"And as He entered a village, He was met by ten lepers, who stood at a distance and lifted up their voices and said, 'Jesus, Master, have mercy on us.' "

— **Luke 17:12-13**

A Tradition of Prayer

How to Make a Prayer of Thanksgiving

Western society has lost the true notion of thankfulness. Yes, we set aside a day once a year when we try to focus on being grateful. Most children are still taught to say "please" and "thank you." Still, we have been so blessed over the last generations that we tend to take for granted our material comforts. Worse yet, many people have begun to view what we have as a "right" rather than a gift. This is not a Christian way of thinking. Good Christians cultivate an "attitude of gratitude."

Prayers of thanksgiving should daily have a place in our relationship to God. "Thanksgiving characterizes the prayer of the Church which, in celebrating the Eucharist, reveals and becomes more fully what she is" (*CCC*, no. 2637). To pray with the Church, to be a Eucharistic people, requires that we be thankful. The word *Eucharist*, literally, means "thanksgiving" in Greek.

There are some gifts of God for which we should be especially thankful. Among them are our families, the sacraments, God's mercy and forgiveness, the Scriptures, and the Church.

Scripture directs us: "[Give] thanks always and for everything in the name of the Lord Jesus to God the Father" (Eph 5:20). And: "Persevere in prayer, being watchful in it with thanksgiving" (Col 4:2). Scripture also gives us many prayers that we can use in thanksgiving. Good starters can be found in Psalms 107, 136, 138, 145, and 147.

We can also simply say "thank you" whenever good things come our way — and even when trials come our way. For all things work together for the good of those who love God. When we cultivate the habit of saying "thank you" to God, we'll see that other virtues follow afterward. Humility, for example, comes more easily to someone who is grateful, who sees himself always on the receiving end of God's favors.

Consider This

We easily accept that it is appropriate to give thanks when we experience blessings. But spiritual writers tell us that our gratitude needs to go beyond this. Scripture, when speaking of thanksgiving, includes such phrases as "in all circumstances" and "at all times." Even when we are in the midst of struggle or hardship, God is still with us. He still cares for us, even when we don't readily sense His care. Thus, it is appropriate to thank God even amid difficulties and trials. Praying a prayer of thanksgiving at these times not only attests to the reality of God's love and constancy, but it also helps us to have the right perspective. We can be secure in the knowledge of our Lord's presence with us.

O Give Thanks

"In all circumstances give thanks, for this is the will of God for you in Christ Jesus."

— 1 Thessalonians 5:18 (NAB)

"From the depths of my heart I thank You, dear Lord, for Your infinite kindness in coming to me! With Your most holy Mother and all the angels, I praise Your mercy and generosity toward me a poor sinner. I thank You for nourishing my soul with Your Sacred Body and Blood. I will try to show my gratitude to You in the Sacrament of Your love, by obedience to Your holy commandments, by fidelity to my duties, by kindness to my neighbor and by earnest endeavor to become more like You in my daily conduct."

— Prayer of Thanksgiving for the Eucharist

How to Read the Bible

St. John Chrysostom tells us that the Holy Scriptures are letters sent by God to man. Have you been reading your "mail" lately? In the Scriptures, inspired by the Holy Spirit, we learn of God, His ways, and His will for us. St. Jerome tells us that ignorance of the Scriptures is ignorance of Christ.

Reading from the Bible should be a regular part of our devotional life. A little time set aside each day, perhaps in conjunction with a time of prayer, is a wise practice. Our reading should always be done prayerfully. Since it is God's desire to speak to us and form us through His Word, we should have expectant hearts each and every time we pick up the Bible.

If you are not accustomed to reading the Bible, it is important to choose wisely where to begin. Starting with one of the four Gospels is a good beginning. After the Gospels, some of the epistles of St. Paul would be a good next step.

Before you actually begin to read, take a moment to recollect that you are about to take in the living Word of God. Ask the Holy Spirit to guide you and form you as you read. You can do this with your own words or by using a prayer like the one below.

Come, Holy Ghost, fill the hearts of Thy faithful, and enkindle in them the Fire of Thy Love.

Send forth Thy Spirit, and they shall be created; And Thou shalt renew the face of the earth.

Let us pray.

O God, Who by the Light of the Holy Spirit did instruct the hearts of Your faithful, grant us in that same Spirit to be truly wise and ever to rejoice in His consolations, through Christ Our Lord. Amen.

Then read slowly and let the words penetrate your thoughts and heart. Scripture is a precious gift from God, and it should be savored.

We should also approach Scripture with a humble heart. God will speak to us through His word, but our knowledge and understanding are limited. We best apply the word of God to our lives with the help of spiritual direction. Personal interpretation must always yield in obedience to the teaching of the Church. It is the Church that has been appointed the protector of God's Word and, by the guidance of the Holy Spirit, the final interpreter of the Word.

There are many translations of the Scripture, but only certain versions are approved for liturgical use in the Church. Since these versions have been scrutinized by Church authorities for accuracy of translation, it is best to use these versions for personal devotion as well. You should also know that not all Christians accept the full text of the Bible as the tradition has preserved it for us. It is best to find a Bible that is explicitly Catholic. Sometimes you can tell by the words on the cover; sometimes you can tell by the presence of an "Imprimatur," or statement of Church approval, on the Bible's copyright page.

Some people use the daily readings from the Mass as their daily scriptural reading. Doing this can help us to participate more fully in the Church's liturgical life.

Hold That Thought

A religion teacher wanted to impress upon his students the value of God's word in the Bible. He told them that the book was useless unless it was used. "If a passage of Scripture touches you," he said, "tear it out of the book and carry it with you and read it regularly." We don't necessarily need to destroy a book, but the idea of carrying Scripture with us is a good idea. There are pocket New Testaments that fit easily into a coat, a briefcase, or a purse. How often do you find yourself waiting — for a bus, for your doctor, for someone to pick up a phone? What a wonderful opportunity to take out your New Testament and read a few passages.

The Bible can also be invaluable in family devotions. To read a short passage, perhaps from the Book of Proverbs or the Psalms, at the end of a meal, will help family members grow in knowledge and appreciation of Scripture.

The Word of God

"Here we are going to read the words, not of a lord of this world, but of the Prince of Angels. If we prepare ourselves in this manner, the grace of the Holy Spirit will guide us with all certainty and we will reach the very throne of the King, and we will attain all good things through the grace and love of Our Lord Jesus Christ, to whom be the glory and power, with the Father and the Holy Spirit, now and forever. Amen."

— St. John Chrysostom

"Read very often the divine Scriptures; never abandon the sacred reading."

— St. John Chrysostom

"Divine Scripture is like a field in which we are going to build a house. We cannot be lazy and be happy to build just on the surface: we have to dig down until we reach the living rock, and this rock is Christ."

— St. Augustine

How to Practice "Mental Prayer"

Have you noticed how some longtime friends can communicate without words? A gesture, a glance, a movement conveys all the information they need. The truth told in a handshake or an embrace perhaps could never be put into words.

In our relationship with God, our words are invaluable. But they are not everything. Our recited, formal prayer is sometimes called "vocal prayer." There is another kind of prayer that is offered in silence. For vocal prayer has its limits, and sometimes words and forms can be more of an obstacle than a help. In addition to vocal prayer, we must also communicate with God in a way that does not primarily depend on words.

This is "mental prayer." In mental prayer, the mind and heart do the work of communication. Perhaps this sounds exotic, but it really shouldn't. You've probably already experienced mental prayer without being fully aware of it. Perhaps you were trying to understand the seemingly senseless suffering of a friend, and you found yourself mentally raising the situation up to God, asking Him to give you light.

Or maybe you experienced mental prayer while looking at a crucifix. You began to think about the sacrifice of Jesus — that He became a man and bore our sins. You considered the love He showed to you in submitting Himself to men and carrying the cross. As you considered those facts, your heart stirred with love. Your affections reached out to embrace the God Who has done so much for you. This is mental prayer. Although words may play a part, it is your mind, heart, and will that communicate directly with God.

Another example: It is right before Communion at Mass. As you pray the "Lamb of God" you are struck by

"As the eyes of a maid to the hand of her mistress,
So our eyes look to the Lord our God."

— Psalm 123:1-2

---

your unworthiness to receive the all-holy God. You heart again is moved to revulsion toward your sins and gratitude for the mercy of God. As you consider God's love for you, your affections "speak" love to Him. You experience a strong desire to be more faithful. Almost imperceptibly you recommit yourself to God.

Mental prayer is the conversation with God that takes place in the quiet of your own mind and heart. It is more than running down a mental list of gratitudes and grievances; it is speaking one's mind, speaking from the heart — and it is giving God the time and the silence to answer you in the depths of your soul.

Mental prayer is something we can cultivate. Sometimes, it just seems to "happen," as in the above examples. For, in all prayer, God is taking the initiative. We enter into the communication that He has already begun. Yet we should never see prayer as a passive activity. We can set specific times when we engage in mental prayer. During these times we specifically turn our hearts and minds to God. At the beginning of our time of mental prayer, we make an act of the will, giving our full attention to God. We acknowledge His presence and His love. Then we open our thoughts to God and allow our heart to respond. We are moved to godly intent, decisions, and action. This type of focused mental prayer is sometimes called "meditation" and will be discussed in greater detail in the next chapter.

We have said on several occasions that prayer is a two-way relationship — God speaks to man and man speaks to God. Often the question is: "How do I hear God?" It probably won't be by audible words. Yet, we can and should expect to "hear" God in our mental prayer.

Consider the one person to whom you are closest. Don't you sometimes communicate without words — by a smile, a wink, a nudge? Some communication transcends words. Communication from God to us *normally* transcends words. Moreover, communication from God normally transcends the senses of sight and touch as well. That link between you and your friend, although deeper than words, still depends on the senses. Your communication with God, on the other hand, can go beyond all senses. He can communicate fully at the level of heart and mind.

Most people have experienced this to some degree. For example, you may be prayerfully reading a passage from the Bible when some line seems to jump off the page. You experience urgency about the passage, or you come to a new level of understanding. Is it merely your mind working on the Scripture? Maybe, but it is also quite possible that the new insight has its origin in the Holy Spirit working within you — God speaking to your heart and mind.

At other times, maybe, you've prayed intensely about something, but received no discernible answer to your prayers. Then, days or weeks later, while you are going about your business, you suddenly "see" the solution you had sought weeks before in prayer. It is entirely possible that God had "planted" His response in your soul during your prayer, only to have it "blossom" in season.

Hearing is a sense that functions automatically. Truly

"Those that seek shall find; and finding Him they will praise Him."

— **St. Augustine**

listening, however, requires a conscious effort on our part. When a teacher speaks to us, we need to pay attention, focus, and integrate what we hear into our experience and understanding. It is the same way with nonverbal communication. We learn over time what our friend means by a certain facial expression or action. The parallel continues in our relationship with God. We need to be active listeners when we pray. We need to learn to sense the movement of His Spirit in our hearts and minds. This comes only by our sustained, disciplined, loving, and faithful efforts at prayer. Mental prayer grows as we develop a deeper relationship with God; our relationship with God grows deeper as we remain faithful to spending time with Him in mental prayer.

Consider This

Inner silence, reflection, and stillness of spirit are essential components of mental prayer. These are commodities that are often difficult to find in our busy days. There are many demands on our time and energies. We must often fight for the opportunity to practice regular mental prayer. Setting a fixed time is very helpful. First thing in the morning is often the best time, because we are rested physically and our minds are relatively uncluttered. The concerns of the day have not begun to consume our thoughts. But, for some people, the time immediately after work provides the best opportunity for mental prayer. Use this simple rule as your guide: The best time for you to pray is the time when you'll pray. Consider your circumstances and your own mental rhythms; then set a time that works for you.

The right place is also important. There is no better place for mental prayer than before Our Lord in the tabernacle. Twenty minutes of daily, quiet meditation and mental prayer before the tabernacle is a powerful practice that will certainly strengthen your relationship with Jesus. If time in church is simply impossible, then a quiet room at your home or workplace may suit you.

We said that mental prayer is an opportunity to "hear" God speaking to us or to gain a sense of how He is working in our lives. We must raise a caution here. First, we should always remember that God reveals Himself to those who seek Him. Jesus sent the Holy Spirit to guide us in the way of truth. So it's healthy to expect that God will communicate with us. But we should always temper that expectation with humility. We are all subject to deception. Even in prayer, we can deceive ourselves or we can allow the devil to deceive us. Mental prayer, like all forms of prayer and devotion, fits into an overall plan of life (more on this later). Spiritual direction can help us best discern what God is saying to us.

"Crying to the Lord is not done with the physical voice, but with the heart. Many whose lips are silent cry out with the heart; many are noisy with their mouths but with their hearts averted are able to obtain nothing. If, then, you cry out to God, cry out inwardly where He hears you."

— **St. Augustine**

Conversations With God

"As the deer longs for streams of water, so my soul
longs for You, O God.
My being thirsts for God, the living God. When can
I go and see the face of God?"

— Psalm 42:2-3

"Mental prayer . . . is the soul's personal contact with
God. It is our private audience with God."

— Rev. Frederick T. Hoeger

"Who can doubt but that cries raised to the Lord in
prayer sound in vain if uttered only with the voice of the
body and not with the heart fixed on God? But, if they
come from the heart, then, they may escape any other
man's notice if the physical voice be silent, but they will
not escape the notice of God. Therefore, whether we cry
to the Lord with the voice of the body — when occasion
demands it — or in silence, we must cry from the heart."

— St. Augustine

"To Thee I lift up my eyes,
O Thou Who art enthroned in the heavens!
Behold, as the eyes of the servants look to the hand
of their master,
As the eyes of a maid to the hand of her mistress,
So our eyes look to the LORD our God."

— Psalm 123:1-2

How to Meditate

Meditation is an important and fundamental form of mental prayer. Since it is "mental," it involves our mind and will. The *Catechism of the Catholic Church* defines meditation as "a prayerful quest engaging thought, imagination, emotion, and desire. Its goal is to make our own, in faith, the subject considered, by confronting it with the reality of our own life" (no. 2723).

This is a powerful definition; and each word is packed with meaning. "A quest" conveys the sense of seeking, pursuing an honorable goal. Like a medieval knight, the believer on a quest needs vigor, determination, and purpose. The goal is to "know Jesus Christ." As St. Paul says in his letter to the Philippians: "I count everything as loss because of the surpassing worth of knowing Christ Jesus my Lord . . . I press on toward the goal for the prize of the upward call of God in Christ Jesus. Let those of us who are mature be thus minded" (Phil 3:8, 14-15).

Meditation is that pursuit of God, His ways, and His "upward call." It involves the use of thought, imagination, emotion, and desire. Many people begin meditation by the use of some spiritual book, and there is no better instrument to use in beginning meditation than the New Testament.

You might begin your time of meditation by acknowledging God's presence and asking for the guidance of the Holy Spirit. Next, read a short portion of the Scripture — just a few lines at most. Then prayerfully consider that passage with the realization that God wishes to lead you in the ways of life. There are many ways to approach this consideration. You might imagine what it would be like to be one of the participants in the scriptural drama. Or you might imagine that you are present there as an observer. You can also consider the impact of the scene on

"Whoever aims at arriving at interior and spiritual things, must, with Jesus, go aside from the crowd."

— St. Thomas Aquinas

---

the salvation of mankind — on your own salvation and that of your friends and family. Turn the passage over in your mind and give it the opportunity to sink in. Gradually, perhaps, you'll see the application of this passage to your life, and you can make appropriate resolutions for future action. In the end, then, your meditation should change the way you think and the way you live.

When, with the help of the Holy Spirit, your mind has finished the slow review of the particular passage of Scripture, you can move on to another short passage and repeat the process. When you have completed the time you had set aside for meditation, give thanks to God for the thoughts and inspirations He has given you in your mediation, and ask for help to implement them in your life.

Other spiritual works can also be used for meditation. Or no books at all. Some people find it useful just to focus on a sacred image of some scene from the life of Christ: a Madonna and Child, or a crucifix. Others find riches just by turning over some mystery of faith, such as the Annunciation of the Angel Gabriel to Mary, or the actions of Jesus at the Last Supper.

Few people have achieved instant success at meditation. To be effective, meditation needs to become a longstanding habit. Sometimes, it will seem easy, exciting, and invigorating. At other times, it will leave us feeling dry and barren. As any medieval knight would tell you, a quest is not all smooth roads and open gates by daylight. But our goal — growth in divine life — is worth the effort. For with that goal come peace, clarity of purpose, lasting friendship — and eternal life. Thus we need to persevere in the practice even if our meditations seem fruitless, labored, or even boring. Humble and prayerful discipline will bring us long-term benefits. As Mother Teresa of Calcutta said again and again: "God does not require success but faithfulness."

Right now, our mind, imagination, and desire all play vital roles in our communication with God. But in heaven we will no longer see dimly in a mirror, but face to face. The saints unanimously teach us that a taste of this intimacy with God is possible for us, even here on earth. Meditation can lead to this deeper form of prayer, which is called contemplation. In meditation, words play a minimal part because the mind and heart are the primary means of communication. In contemplation, the mind and heart play a minimal part, as the lover achieves a union with the Beloved at the level of the spirit.

None of these concepts yield easily to the vocabulary of everyday life. But the entry into contemplative prayer is normally through the channel of sustained and disciplined meditative prayer.

Hold That Thought

Anyone who practices mental prayer and meditation will have to struggle against distraction. If we are not on guard, our time of prayer can easily turn into a session of merely planning our activities or agonizing over our problems. There are several ways to deal with distractions. Sometimes we can view the distraction as a temptation. In that case, we dismiss it, refocus on the Lord, and continue with the meditation. Other times, an impending event will intrude itself upon our thoughts. Here, perhaps, it might be more helpful just to jot down a note for later consideration, so that the urgent matter will no longer be a cause for distraction. Sometimes, we can make the distraction a part of our prayer. Perhaps your concern for a family member is distracting you from meditation on a scriptural passage. Take the occasion to pray for that person — maybe in the context of what you have just read in Scripture. Entrust the individual to the mercy and love of God and then return to your mediation. If you find that distractions are a regular problem, you may need to change the circumstances of your prayer. A different time or location may help. You should also discuss such difficulties with your spiritual director, confessor, or someone more mature in the faith.

You might also find it helpful to keep a journal. Place a notebook nearby during your meditation. At the end of the time of prayer, make some note on your reflection. What comes to mind could be something that Christ was teaching you. It may be a new insight. It could be a question or a resolution. Over time, as you review your journal, your notes can help you discern what God is telling you and where He may be leading you.

"Prayer is then not just a formula of words, or a series of desires springing up in the heart — it is the orientation of our whole body, mind, and spirit to God in silence, attention, and adoration."

— **Thomas Merton**

In God's Presence

"Seek a proper time to retire into yourself, and often think of the benefits of God . . . . If you will withdraw yourself from superfluous talk and idle visits, and also from giving ear to news and to reports, you will find time sufficient and proper to employ yourself in good meditations."

— **St. Thomas Aquinas**

"Practice meditation for a fixed period and at a fixed time. Otherwise we would be putting our own convenience first."

— **Blessed Josémaria Escrivá**

"(Meditation) is necessary in order that we may have light to go on the journey to eternity. Eternal truths are spiritual things that are not seen by the eyes of the body but only by the reflection of the mind. He who does not mediate does not see them; and thus he advances with difficulty along the way of salvation."

—**St. Alphonsus Liguori**

A prayer after personal meditation:
"Take, O Lord, into Your hands my entire liberty, my memory, my understanding and my will. All that I am and have, You have given me, and I surrender them to You, to be so disposed in accordance with Your holy will. Give me Your love and Your grace; with these I am rich enough and desire nothing more."

— **St. Ignatius of Loyola**

"There Elijah came to a cave, where he took shelter. But the word of the Lord came to him, 'Why are you here, Elijah?' He answered: 'I have been most zealous for the Lord, the God of hosts, but the Israelites have forsaken your covenant, torn down Your altars, and put Your prophets to the sword. I alone am left, and they seek to take my life.' Then the Lord said, 'Go outside and stand on the mountain before the Lord; the Lord will be passing by.' A strong and heavy wind was rending the mountains and crushing rocks before the Lord — but the Lord was not in the wind. After the wind there was an earthquake — but the Lord was not in the earthquake. After the earthquake there was fire — but the Lord was not in the fire. After the fire there was a tiny whispering sound. When he heard this, Elijah hid his face in his cloak and went and stood at the entrance of the cave."

— 1 Kings 19:9-13 (NAB)

How to Pray an Aspiration

(Ejaculation)

God is the source and sustainer of each human life. Breathing is necessary for life. According to Genesis, God breathed life into the dust and created man. We take breathing for granted, but it is one of the essentials of life — a life given by God. Shouldn't we "breathe forth" praise to our creator?

The *American Heritage Dictionary* defines aspiration as "expulsion of breath in speech . . . the act of breathing, inhalation." In the prayer of the Church, this "breathing" has a special definition. An aspiration or ejaculation is a short prayer — just a few words at most — that glorifies God, thanks Him, or petitions Him for help.

A wife as she passes her husband seated in a chair may lean over and whisper: "I love you." There is no long conversation, but that short phrase expresses a deep relationship. Moreover, those three words whispered hastily help the relationship grow deeper still, and more intimate.

By aspirations we breathe forth words of love to God. We speak them when lengthy prayers are not possible or appropriate. They rise from a relationship with God that has already been established. They tap the wealth that is available from the grace or God and hold the promise of the future.

Some examples? A business executive is about to interview a prospective employee. He realizes that God is concerned about every aspect of life. He knows that he needs the grace and guidance of the Holy Spirit. He desires to make good decisions both for the benefit of his company and for the individual who is being interviewed. In the moment before the candidate enters the office door,

"My Lord and my God."

---

the interviewer whispers, repeating the words that the blind man spoke to Jesus in the Bible: "Lord, that I might see!"

A mother has had an exasperating day. The children seem to be fighting constantly. The telephone keeps ringing. She thinks: *I don't know if I can take one more thing.* She stops and whispers: "Jesus, You are my hope and my strength."

A young woman drives past a Catholic church. While still listening to her business associate sitting in the passenger seat, she says in her mind: "Jesus, present in the tabernacle, I love You."

A student, before beginning an exam, makes a small cross on the top of the paper as he quietly prays: "Jesus, my Lord and my Savior."

An aspiration can even be a single word, such as "Lord!" or "Father!" or "Thanks!" or "Help!" or "Jesus!"

On the surface, these prayers may not appear to be profound — no more profound than that spouse's "I love you." Yet aspirations help to build a climate of prayer in our lives. They are a way of renewing our sense that God is with us and hears us. We can ask His help, seek His guidance, ask His forgiveness, thank Him, or merely let Him know of our love for Him. It is simple, yet it is profound. It is life-giving. It is spiritual breathing.

Consider This

The habit of making regular aspirations can help us to fulfill St. Paul's admonition that we pray always. We may spend twenty minutes in mental prayer each day. We may say the Rosary and offer some morning and evening prayers. Aspirations can be a thread we weave to connect all those separate times of prayer.

There are several ways to develop the habit of aspirations. The ordinary places, times, and events of the day can be the impetus for those moments of prayer. For example, if you have a watch that beeps on the hour, you can say an aspiration when you hear the beep.

Use a place to remind you. Every time you walk through a certain doorway, offer a quick prayer. Or when you stop at the water fountain, remember your Baptism and take the opportunity to give God a few words of thanks.

Where do you find the words? Scripture is a good source, and so is the liturgy. Or you can make up your own aspirations. If you sense that God wants you to develop us in some area of your life, you can focus your aspirations on that area. Maybe you've come to the conclusion that God is trying to make you more generous and forgiving. Then your aspiration might relate to that intention: "Lord, make my heart like Yours."

"Lord what do You want me to do?"

—Acts 22:10

In One Breath

- Jesus is Lord.

- Come, Holy Spirit.

- Jesus, Mary, Joseph.

- My Jesus, mercy.

- **Maranatha! Come, Lord Jesus** (Rev 22:20).

- **Create a clean heart in me, O God** (Ps 51:12).

- **A contrite and humble heart, O God, You will not despise** (Ps 51:19).

- All glory to God.

- **My Lord and my God** (John 20:28). *This aspiration was traditionally said silently by Catholics at the elevation of the Body and Blood of Jesus at Mass.*

- **For those who love God, all things work together for good** (Rom 8:28).

- **For you, O Lord, are my strength** (Ps 43:2).

- **He must increase, but I must decrease** (Jn 3:30).

- **Here I am, for You did call me** (1 Sam 3:5).

• Holy Mary, our hope, seat of wisdom, pray for us.

• **I do believe; help my unbelief** (Mk 9:24).

• I give You thanks for all Your benefits, even the unknown ones.

• **In you, O Lord, I take refuge: let me never be put to shame** (Ps 31:1).

• **Jesus, Son of David, have mercy on me a sinner** (Mk 10:47).

• **Lord, increase our faith** (Lk 17:5).

• **Lord, You know all things, you know that I love You** (Jn 21:17).

• **Lord, that I may see** (Lk 18:41).

• **Lord, what do you want me to do?** (Acts 22:10).

• **Not as I will, but as You will** (Mt 26:39).

• Queen of Apostles, pray for us.

• Sacred Heart of Jesus, grant us peace.

• Sweet Heart of Mary, prepare a safe way for us.

• **I can do all things in Him Who strengthens me** (Phil 4:13).

How to Pray to the Saints

"Some of my best friends are saints!" should be among the mottoes of a prayerful Catholic. The saints have made it. They've successfully faced the struggles and temptations of this life. By God's grace, they have triumphed and now worship before the throne of God. We see in the Bible's Book of Revelation that they also remain much aware of life here on earth, and that they offer powerful prayers for those of us who are still struggling.

Thus we can pray to the saints and ask their intercession. For we are united with them in the mystical body of Christ. The Gospel urges us to pray for one another, and we often ask the prayers of those living beside us. To ask the intercession of the saints is merely to acknowledge that life goes on, even after the body dies. Death does not separate us from our brothers and sisters in Christ. Death does not remove a Christian's desire to help others. Thus, we — both those on earth and those in heaven — continue to bow together before God and worship Him Who has created us, saved us, and sustained us.

Why ask the saints to pray for us? First, because they are family. We share close bonds of kinship with the saints in heaven, the souls in purgatory, and all the faithful on earth. Like any good family, we all share a concern for one another. The pain of one member matters to all the others. The joy and the grace of one member are available to be shared by all. When we speak to the saints, we speak with elder family members.

Also, when you have a need, don't you take it to someone you trust? Don't you also seek out someone who understands your problems? The saints fulfill both of these requirements. We can entrust them with our needs and know that they will faithfully bring our needs to God. The saints know our struggles and temptations. They too have experienced them. Some saints may be close to us because of similarity of life or struggle. When we ask for a particular saint's intercession, we speak to someone who has walked our way and emerged victorious.

When we ask for prayer, we normally seek out those who are close to God. We on earth see dimly as in a mirror, but the saints see Our Lord as it were "face to face." They are free from the distractions of this life and their focus is upon the Lord.

The Church has raised up, through the process of canonization, men and women of all ages and from all states of life as examples for us. We're inspired when we see people who resemble us in age, vocation, and temperament, who have been faithful to God. Some saints are designated as "patrons" of particular activities, professions, or groups of people. For example, St. Monica was the mother of a wayward son who drifted from the faith and fell into grievous sin and embraced heretical teaching. She faithfully prayed for this son and patiently encouraged him. Eventually, through her prayers and example, this young man returned to God and became one of the most renowned of the Church Fathers. His name is St. Augustine. Down through the ages, many mothers have asked St. Monica to pray that they too might be good and holy mothers. The example and prayers of St. Monica have brought comfort to many and have led to her designation as a patron of mothers. Also:

• St. Martha, the sister of Mary and Lazarus, offered hospitality to Jesus and His disciples. She is the patron saint of cooks.

• Are you an accountant or a bookkeeper? If so, your patron is St. Matthew, who left the tax collector's table to follow Jesus.

Countries, too, have patron saints. St. Anne and St. Joseph are called upon to watch over Canada. St. Patrick's heart was for Ireland and its people. St. George intercedes for England.

There are patron saints for specific needs and situations. St. Joseph, who died in the arms of Jesus and Mary, is the patron saint of the dying. The intercession of St. Jude is often invoked in desperate, seemingly hopeless situations. And if you've lost something, tradition leads you to St. Anthony of Padua for assistance.

Consider This

We all need examples that inspire us. Young people look for heroes they can emulate. The saints provide that example and inspiration. Reading the lives of the saints can help us to strive more earnestly to obey and follow God. It is helpful to seek out a book about a saint who appeals to you.

In honoring particular saints, we give honor to the source of their virtue — Christ Himself. We must never approach a saint in a superstitious manner. Saints can and do help us, but they do so as the channels of God's grace and mercy. We've all known times when other people, perhaps parents or friends, have been the means of God's blessing us. It is the same with the saints. "Thank you" is an appropriate response when someone — on earth or in heaven — brings grace to us from God. Ultimately, all praise and thanks belong to the source, which is God.

Pray for Us

"Let us remember one another in concord and unanimity. Let us on both sides (of death) always pray for one another."

— St. Cyprian

"It is . . . most useful to us, in order to obtain the divine grace, that we have recourse to the intercession of the saints, who have great power with God, especially for the benefit of those who have a particular devotion to them."

— St. Alphonsus Liguori

"There being a medium of communication between us and the saints, and they and we form one Communion, one body of Our Lord, being members of Him and members of one another, nothing can be more reasonable, more natural even, than that we should invoke their prayers, and that they should intercede for us."

— Orestes A. Brownson

"The twenty-four elders fell down before the Lamb. Each of the elders held a harp and gold bowls filled with incense, which are the prayers of the holy ones."

— Revelation 5:8 (NAB)

A Selection
of Prayers to Saints:

To St. Joseph for a Happy Death

O Blessed St. Joseph, who died in the arms of Jesus and Mary, obtain for me, I beseech you, the grace of a happy death. In that hour of dread and anguish, assist me by your power against the enemies of my salvation. Into your hands, living and dying, Jesus, Mary, and Joseph, I commend my soul. Amen.

To St. Anthony

Blessed St. Anthony, you are the gentlest of saints, your love for God and charity for His creatures made you worthy, when on earth, to possess miraculous powers. Miracles waited on your word, which you were ever ready to speak for those in trouble or anxiety. Encouraged by this thought, I implore you to obtain for me (*mention your request here*). The answer to my prayer may require a miracle; even so you are the Saint of Miracles. O gentle, and loving saint, whose heart was ever full of human sympathy, intercede for me to Jesus. You who so loved the word of God and are a Doctor of the Gospel, ask that "it be done to me according to His word," and the gratitude of my heart will ever be yours.

To St. Jude

Glorious St. Jude, with faith in your goodness, we ask your help today. As one of Christ's chosen apostles, you remain a pillar and foundation of His Church on earth. You are counted, we know, among the elders who always stand before God's throne.

From your place of glory we know you do not forget the needs and difficulties of Christ's little ones here, still struggling, like me, on the way home to God. Please intercede for us all, gracious St. Jude, and be with us in our daily toil and in our necessities. In Christ's name, we appeal to you again today. Amen.

— Franciscan Mission Associates

To St. Thérèse of the Child Jesus

O wondrous St. Thérèse of the Child Jesus, who, in your brief earthly life, became a mirror of angelic purity, of courageous love and wholehearted surrender to Almighty God, now that you enjoy the reward of your virtues, turn your eyes of mercy upon us who trust in you. Obtain for us the grace to keep our hearts and minds pure and clean like yours, and to detest in all sincerity whatever might tarnish ever so slightly the luster of a virtue so sublime, a virtue that endears us to your heavenly Bridegroom. Dear saint, grant us to feel in every need the power of your intercession; give us comfort in all the bitterness of this life and especially at its latter end, that we may be worthy to share eternal happiness with you in paradise. Amen.

— From *My Catholic Devotions*

How to Pray to Angels

Some scientists dedicate their life to studying whether there are intelligent beings, other than humans, in the universe. A Christian knows that there are other intelligent beings, and we call them angels. They are mentioned in no less than two hundred verses of the Bible. From Scripture we can determine three functions of angelic beings.

Primarily these pure spirits serve in the heavenly court and worship at God's throne. There are not many direct quotations that are attributed to angels, but one tells us the words they spoke on the first Christmas. Angels appeared in the sky and proclaimed: "Glory to God in the highest!" (Lk 2:14).

So, above all, our conversation with angels is related to their most important duty. We are called to join them in their praise. In the Mass we hear the words of the priest: "We join with all the choirs of heaven as they sing forever to Your glory." That chorus is never ending. We have the opportunity to add our voice to the chorus of praise: "Holy, holy, holy Lord," the song sung by the angels in both the Old Testament and the New. If we wish to improve our concentration in praise and worship, we should ask the help of the experts: the angels.

The name "angel" means messenger, and the Bible provides many examples of angels serving God as messengers to humans. Yet, only three of the angels' names are revealed in Scripture. Gabriel, whose name means "The Power of God," first appeared in the Book of Daniel, but he is best know as the messenger who announced to Mary that she was chosen to be the mother of the Savior.

The Archangel Michael's name means "Who Is Like God?" Michael took his name seriously as he led the obedient angels in the battle against Lucifer and the rebellious angels (see Rev 12:7). In the Book of Daniel, Michael is called the "Guardian of the People." Michael is often invoked for protection against the attacks of the devil.

Raphael is only named in the Old Testament. He brought God's healing and guidance to Tobit, Tobias, and Sarah, as recorded in the book of Tobit. His name means "God Heals." It is appropriate to ask his help and guidance in discerning God's will in your life.

The angels who have the most daily impact on our lives are our guardian angels. Of these angels, the *Catechism* states: "From infancy to death human life is surrounded by their watchful care and intercession. 'Beside each believer stands an angel as protector and shepherd leading him to life.' Already here on earth the Christian life shares by faith in the blessed company of angels and men united in God" (no. 336).

We should, then, keep an active, ongoing prayer relationship with our own guardian angel. We can ask our angel to watch over us, guide us, and protect us.

This conversation need not be limited to our own guardian angels. Whenever our physical eyes see an individual, our spirit should realize that two beings stand there. One is a human person and the other is the angel assigned to guard that man or woman. If we cultivate the habit of silently greeting everyone's guardian angel, we can be sure that we will experience growth not only in our spiritual life, but in our human relationships. The angels of our friends, acquaintances, and co-workers will help us to maintain good, peaceful dealings with everyone.

"The angel of the Lord encamps around those who fear him, and delivers them."

— **Psalm 34:7**

Hold That Thought

Your angel is assigned to help you, but is limited by your free will. God never forces Himself on you; nor does your guardian angel. When you actively ask the assistance of your angel, you, in effect, authorize the activity and power of that angel. Remember that, wherever you go, you take your guardian angel. So before you go anywhere, ask yourself if it is a proper place for an angel to go! It can help you to avoid places of temptation.

Angels Watching Over Me

" 'He has given His angels charge over you to guard you in all your ways' (Ps 91). These words should fill you with respect, inspire devotion and instill confidence; respect for the presence of angels, devotion because of their loving service, and confidence because of their protection."

— St. Bernard

"See, I [the Lord] am sending an angel before you, to guard you on the way and bring you to the place I have prepared."

— Exodus 23:20 (NAB)

"See that you do not despise one of these little ones, for I say to you that their angels in heaven always look upon the face of my heavenly Father."

— Matthew 18:10 (NAB)

Prayers to Angels

Guardian Angel

Angel of God, my guardian dear, to whom God's love commits me here; ever this day (or night) be at my side, to light and guard, to rule and guide. Amen.

Children's Prayer

Guardian angel from heaven so bright, watching beside me to lead me aright, fold your wings around me, and guard me with love, softly sing songs to me of heaven above. Amen.

Prayer to St. Michael

St. Michael the archangel, defend us in battle. Be our protection against the wickedness and snares of the devil. May God rebuke him we humbly pray, and do thou, O prince of the heavenly host, by the power of God, thrust into hell Satan and all evil spirits who prowl about the world seeking the ruin of souls. Amen.

". . . The angels must be closely akin to us, for otherwise God would not have used them as our guardians."

— J. P. Arendzen

How to Observe First Fridays and First Saturdays

In the thirteenth century arose a devotion to Jesus and Mary under the titles of the "Sacred Heart of Jesus" and the "Immaculate Heart of Mary." The heart is the source and center of life, and life flows out to the faithful from the hearts of Jesus and Mary. St. Bonaventure focused in particular on the wound that Jesus received from the spear of the Roman centurion. From that wound, blood and water flowed — a sign that Jesus gave everything for us (Jn 19:34). Devotion to the heart of Mary draws from the Gospel of Luke (2:35), in which Simeon tells Mary, "Your own soul a sword shall pierce." Simeon prophesied that Mary would share in the sufferings of her Son and Redeemer, Jesus.

In the seventeenth century, St. John Eudes promoted these devotions. He also developed Mass texts and daily readings focused on the Sacred Heart of Jesus and the Admirable Heart of Mary. He proposed that both be made into feasts in the Church's liturgical calendar.

As the Devotion to the Sacred Heart spread, a cloistered nun, Sister Margaret Mary Alacoque, received a series of visions. Christ Himself directed St. Margaret Mary to spread devotion to His Sacred Heart. One of these devotions was to make the first Friday of each month a special day of devotion. Specifically, the devotion involved receiving Holy Communion on nine consecutive first Fridays. Those observing the devotion were to do so with the intention of reparation to "the Heart that has loved men so and is loved so little in return." Jesus told St. Margaret Mary of His great love for souls and His desire to shower His mercy on those who were devoted to Him. He revealed several promises for those who lovingly practiced the First Friday devotion. Among the promises were: final perseverance in the Catholic faith, reception of the sacraments before death, and death in the state of grace, as well as the consolation of Christ's love at the time of death.

Devotion to the Immaculate Heart of Mary developed alongside the devotion to the Sacred Heart of Jesus. The heart of Mary mirrors the heart of Jesus both in great love and in sharing His suffering. This devotion increased after the appearances of the Blessed Mother to three children of Fátima, Portugal, early in the twentieth century. The Blessed Mother told the eldest of the children that she would "assist at the hour of death with all the graces necessary for the salvation of their souls" all who, for five months, on the first Saturday of each month:

- confess their sins,
- receive Holy Communion,
- recite the Rosary,
- and keep Mary company for fifteen minutes while meditating on the fifteen mysteries of the Rosary,
- all offered in a spirit of reparation.

Of course, all of this assumes the context of a prayerful life and the struggle for holiness. It would be blasphemy to approach the hearts of Jesus and Mary in supplication while fully intending to continue a life of sin.

Hold That Thought

We want to mirror the heart and mind of God. We want to see people, the world, and every situation with God's eyes. We want to love as He loves. We want a heart like His. If we have such a heart, we will begin to love as God loves; yet we will also begin to know how much God is offended by the sins of the world. Then, with such love joined to such a horror of sin, we will want to make reparation for our sins and the sins of others. This is the way that Jesus and Mary loved: by offering their lives to atone for the failings of others.

As we meditate on the hearts of Jesus and Mary, we see the great love they have, even for sinners, and we see how God continues to reach out in love and forgiveness. But we also see how poorly people respond to this loving invitation to life and relationship with God. Some go so far as to actively reject God. We begin to obtain a glimpse of the injustice of habitual sin, which rejects God and abuses His mercy.

The suffering and rejection of the cross continues, but the mercy and grace of God continue to flow to men and women in our time.

Jesus and Mary, make our hearts like yours!

Prayers

To Be United with the Heart of Jesus

O Heart all lovable and all loving of my Savior, be the Heart of my heart, the soul of my soul, the spirit of my spirit, the life of my life and the sole principle of all my thoughts, words and actions, of all the faculties of my soul, and of all my senses, both interior and exterior. Amen.

— St. John Eudes

A Prayer of Adoration

From the depth of my nothingness, I prostrate myself before You, O Most Sacred, Divine and Adorable Heart of Jesus, to pay to You all the homage of love, praise, and adoration in my power. Amen.

—St. Margaret Mary Alacoque

Collect for the
Feast of the Sacred Heart

O Father of mercies and God of all consolation, Who by the exceeding love with which You have loved us, have given us, with ineffable goodness, the Heart of Your Beloved Son, so that having but one heart with Him we may love You perfectly; grant, we beseech You, that our hearts, being consumed in unity with the Heart of Jesus and with one another, we may perform all our works in accord with His humility and charity and that by His mediation the just desires of our hearts may be accomplished, through the same Lord. Amen.

To the Immaculate Heart of Mary

O Sorrowful and Immaculate Heart of Mary, Queen of the Most Holy Rosary, and Queen of the World, rule over us, together with the Sacred Heart of Jesus Christ, Our King. Save us from the spreading flood of modern paganism; kindle in our hearts and homes the love of purity, the practice of a virtuous life, an ardent zeal for souls, and a desire to pray the Rosary more faithfully.

How to Help the Dying

Our culture is uncomfortable with death. We don't want to think about it, and we don't want to talk about it. But people of faith know that life does not end when the heart stops beating; life is merely changed. We are destined for eternal life in heaven in a glorious, loving relationship with God — or we are destined for eternal damnation in the self-inflicted punishment resulting from the rejection of God. As C. S. Lewis said, we are destined to become either "immortal horrors or everlasting splendors."

Each of us will eventually be confronted with the reality of death. What should we do when people we know and love are faced with their own imminent death?

Of course, we should pray for anyone who is seriously sick. We should pray for healing, but also pray for acceptance of God's will and for His mercy. It is important to help those who are dying to prepare themselves to meet Our Lord after death. Yet we will often be tempted not to discuss death with people who are seriously ill, out of a concern that we may "upset" them. But it is far worse for a dying person to be spiritually unprepared for death than to be temporarily agitated by the thought of death. So we should not be afraid to broach the subject. We should even offer to call a priest to administer the Sacrament of the Sick. We can assure the grievously sick person that reception of the sacrament does not necessarily mean that end is near. On the contrary, it is prudent to receive the anointing far before death is "at the doorstep." The sacrament is the Church's prayer and anointing for strength in struggle. Thus it is appropriate for those who are ill, but especially for those who may be dying.

A priest who visits someone in danger of death will offer the sick person three sacraments. First comes the opportunity for confession. The greatest gift we can give to someone who is dying is the opportunity to repair their relationship with God. Sincere confession of mortal sin brings forgiveness and opens the doors of heaven. Thus confession is rightly called "the Sacrament of Reconciliation." And the dying can go in peace when they know that they have been reconciled with God.

The priest will also administer the Sacrament of the Anointing of the Sick. He will use the oil that ordinarily has been blessed by the bishop on Holy Thursday. The priest will anoint the sick person on the forehead while praying: "Through this holy anointing, may the Lord in His love and mercy help you with the grace of the Holy Spirit." Those present should respond with: "Amen." He then takes the palms of each hand and traces a Sign of the Cross with the oil saying: "May the Lord who frees you from sin save you and raise you up." Again those present respond: "Amen."

The "raising up" of the prayer may mean physical healing or strengthening but also recalls the hope of the resurrection. The primary intent of the sacrament is spiritual. First there is pardoning of venial sins and any remnants of sin on the soul. The anointing also stirs the recipient to faith in God's mercy and provides a spiritual strengthening to endure suffering. Often the individual will experience a new sense of peace and courage to persevere through suffering.

Finally the priest will give the dying person the opportunity to receive Our Lord Jesus in Communion. This Communion is called "Viaticum" — the Communion for the journey from this life to eternity.

"Is anyone among you sick? He should summon the presbyters of the church and they should pray over him and anoint him with oil in the name of the Lord. . . ."

— James 5:14

91

Consider This

George was dying of cancer. He knew it, and his family knew it. But no one wanted to admit it or talk about it. Even though they were transferring him to hospice care, they still spoke of it as a temporary step until George "got better." A casual friend visited George shortly before he entered the hospice facility. The friend asked George if he felt that he was prepared to die. He also offered to contact a priest if George wished. The dying man grabbed his friend by the arm and began to thank him profusely. "You're the first one who has been willing to talk to me about dying. Yes, I want to see the priest. Can you make the call for me?" The friend made the call and the priest came and administered the sacraments for the dying. Within a few days, George died. In the end, George was extremely grateful to his friend — perhaps eternally grateful.

We need to overcome any timidity and fear about offering to call a priest for a seriously ill person. We should be tactful but direct. For some there will be physical healing, but the spiritual healing of the sacrament is a grace that everyone needs in preparing for death.

A Prayer for the Dying

Most Merciful Jesus, lover of souls, I pray You, by the agony of Your Most Sacred Heart and by the sorrows of Your Immaculate Mother, to wash in Your Most Precious Blood the sinners of the world who are now in their agony, and who will die today. Heart of Jesus, once in agony, have mercy on the dying. Amen.

The End of Earthly Days

"Concerning the departing, the ancient canonical law is still to be maintained, to wit, that, if any man be at the point of death, he must not be deprived of the last and most indispensable Viaticum."

— First Council of Nicaea

"In addition to the Anointing of the Sick, the Church offers those who are about to leave this life the Eucharist as viaticum. Communion in the Body and Blood of Christ, received at this moment of 'passing over' to the Father, has a particular significance and importance. It is the seed of eternal life and the power of resurrection, according to the words of the Lord: 'He who eats my flesh and drinks my blood has eternal life, and I will raise him up at the last day.' The sacrament of Christ once dead and now risen, the Eucharist is here the sacrament of passing over from death to life, from this world to the Father."

— CCC, no. 1524

"It can be said that Penance, the Anointing of the Sick, and the Eucharist as viaticum constitute at the end of Christian life 'the sacraments that prepare for our heavenly homeland' or the sacraments that complete the earthly pilgrimage."

— CCC, no. 1525

How to Pray for the Dead

Look in the bulletin of a typical parish church, and you'll see a schedule of Masses, requested by parishioners and offered for "the repose of the soul" of individuals who have died. Visit a cemetery, and you'll notice the letters "R.I.P." — for "Rest in Peace" — on older tombstones.

What good does it do to wish repose for someone already dead — and even to pray and offer Masses for their sake?

Plenty. St. Paul taught that all believers are united as the "body of Christ": "We, though many, are one body in Christ and individually parts of one another" (Rom 12:5; see also Eph 1-2). If Christ has just one body, then that body must include all the faithful: those in heaven, on earth, and in purgatory.

We each need to love and care for the other members of the body. Like St. Paul, we can make up in our flesh what is lacking in the suffering of Christ, for the sake of His body, the Church (see Col 1:24). In other words, Jesus allows us to participate with Him in the redemption of others. We do this naturally when we pray for people still with us on earth, when we offer sacrifices for their sake, and when we share our faith with them.

But we can also perform acts of love for those who have died. Why do the faithful departed need prayer? Actually, not all of them do. The saints in heaven no longer need our prayers, because they fully enjoy the presence of God. Those who have died estranged from God in mortal sin are also beyond the help of our prayers, for they have sealed their fate by the free choices they made in life — they are condemned to hell.

Still, many people die in God's grace, and by His mercy will enjoy eternal salvation — though not before they are purified. We see in the Book of Revelation (21:27) that nothing impure can enter heaven. Yet, we know that all of us are stained by sin. Does that mean that heaven is an impossible goal? No, but it does mean we must be purified before we can approach the throne of God. That time of purification after death is purgatory. And, by our prayers, we can ease this cleansing process for others.

Praying for the dead is a duty we should gladly fulfill, using traditional prayers or words we ourselves compose. Our first responsibility is to those whom God has given us as family members, friends, and benefactors. But, as we are also called to care for the poor on earth, we should also pray for those in purgatory who are forgotten and have no one else to pray for them.

In a later chapter, we will discuss how to make sacrifices for the intentions of others. The faithful departed can also be the beneficiaries of our sacrifices.

By far the greatest gift we can give to a deceased friend is to have the Holy Sacrifice of the Mass offered for his or her intention. You can do this by contacting your local parish and requesting a Mass for your departed. A small financial offering to the Church is customary. Many mission societies and religious houses will also accept Mass intentions.

"It is a good and wholesome thought to pray for the dead, that they may be loosed from their sins."

— 2 Maccabees 12:45

Consider This

There are two times a year we should particularly focus on prayer for the faithful departed. Once is on All Souls Day, November 2. In the United States, a second day that naturally leads us to think of the departed is the secular holiday of Memorial Day. Both are ideal times to take a family trip to the cemetery and offer prayers for the repose of the souls of loved ones. Many people will also take the opportunity to place flowers or a wreath at the grave as a sign of the continuing love for the deceased. To add prayer for that departed family member expresses that love in a way that is effective. There is no better method of expressing our love than prayer.

Praying for the Dead

"Bury my body wherever you will . . . One thing only I ask you, that you remember me at the altar of the Lord wherever you may be."

— St. Monica

"St. Thomas teaches that Christian charity extends not only to the living but also to all who have died in the state of grace. Hence, as we are bound to relieve our living neighbors who require our aid, so we are obliged to comfort these holy prisoners."

— St. Alphonsus Liguori

Prayer for All the Dead

Accept this prayer which I offer You, merciful Father, for those who have died, those who have gone before us marked with the sign of faith, and those whose faith in this life was known to You alone. Have mercy on them all and bring them into Your kingdom of peace and light without end where You and Your saints live in the happiness which this world has not known and cannot give. Amen.

Prayer for Parents

Merciful Father, it is Your will that all of us share in Your divine life, through the sufferings and death of Jesus, Your Son, Our Lord and Redeemer. I pray to You now for my parents asking for them, through Your mercy and love, a place of eternal rest and never-ending happiness. In life they made many sacrifices for me. In death, I commend their souls to You, Father, to reward them as You alone can with a heavenly home in the presence of You and the saints forever. Amen.

Praying With Mary

How to Pray to Mary

Why does a child cry out for his mother when he's in distress? Why does a little girl pick wildflowers to give as a crumpled bouquet to her mom? We all know that there is a special relationship between a mother and her children.

Why do we pray to Mary and ask her intercession? Why do we honor her above all other saints? Because as members of the family of God, we children know the importance of our Mother.

Eve was the "mother of all the living" according to the physical order. We received life through her; but we also received the effect of the sin of our first parents. We can be sure that we are their descendants because we bear the "genetic" tendency to sin. We call this original sin.

But, praise God, another mother has been given to us in the spiritual order. Mary gave birth to Jesus and is rightly called the "Mother of God." With Jesus, God became man — the "new Adam" — and established a new order in creation. Scripture tells us that "Jesus is the first of many brothers." *We are those brothers of Christ!* As Jesus' brothers and sisters, we come to share everything that is His.

We share His Father: God. We share His family: the Church. And we share His mother: Mary.

One of Jesus' last actions from the cross was to give her to us as our mother. The event is recorded in St. John's Gospel (19:26-27). Jesus looked at His mother, who was standing with His "beloved disciple." Jesus told His Mother: "Woman, behold your son!" To the disciple He said: "Behold, your mother!"

Mary, then, became the mother of all beloved disciples. The arms of the cross spread across time and history. We also are beloved disciples of Christ who stand at the foot of the cross. Christ says to us: "Behold your mother."

Every child must obey the commandment to honor father and mother. Thus, Mary, as our mother in Christ, deserves our most profound respect. The honor we give to her is honor and respect given to her Son, Jesus, Who bestowed every gift upon her. The honor we give to Mary is greater than the honor accorded to any of the angels and saints.

Through Marian prayer, we pay homage to Mary, but we also invoke her power as an intercessor before almighty God. The Gospel shows us that Our Lord will not, after all, refuse His mother (see Jn 2:1-11). The tradition of Marian prayer is rich and varied, from the simple Hail Mary to the longer Litany of Loretto, which is a loving recitation of the many titles that honor the Blessed Mother. The Rosary, which involves recitation of Hail Marys and other prayers, is perhaps the world's most popular form of meditation. The Church sets the entire month of May aside to honor Mary in a special way, with May crownings and other displays of devotion.

How do we begin a prayer to Mary? To have a statute or picture of the Blessed Mother before you can assist you to focus your thoughts. Then open your heart and mind to your mother. Tell her your cares and concerns, and allow her maternal love to comfort you. Ask her to intercede for you with her son, Jesus. As she did at the wedding feast of Cana, Mary will approach her Son. The fruit of that intervention of Mary at Cana was an answer to prayer. Jesus heard and responded — the results will be no less for us.

God's family is perfect, lacking nothing — certainly not someone as important as a mother. Mary loves us, her children, as she loved Jesus, her Child. She loves as only a mother can love, and she loves perfectly, without the hindrance of sin. We can bring our needs and concerns to our mother and ask for her guidance and help. This in no way detracts from Christ or His role as Redeemer. Indeed, it is an acknowledgment of the effectiveness of His saving work and of His desire for each of us to participate in that work. Mary, who fully cooperated with Christ in life, continues to cooperate in Christ's saving plan by assisting us today.

Hold That Thought

We can ask Mary's intercession for any need. Yet there are some areas where we may want to particularly ask Mary's intercession. Since Mary freely, willingly, and fully followed God's will for her life, we should seek her help whenever we are struggling to know or follow God's will. Mary also was the exemplar of purity. Some people make it a practice each day to say three Hail Marys for the intention of maintaining purity in their lives and in the lives of their family members.

Many a priest will credit the Blessed Mother with his ability to respond to his vocation. Mary, who completely submitted to God's will, wants to help young people discern their call from God.

As wife and mother, too, Mary knew many trials and hardships. She knows the struggles of family life. Thus she is a powerful help and intercessor for every wife and mother.

Marian Prayers

Memorare

Remember, most loving Virgin Mary, never was it heard that anyone who turned to you for help was left unaided. Inspired by this confidence, though burdened by my sins, I run to your protection for you are my mother. Mother of the Word of God, do not despise my words of pleading but be merciful and hear my prayer. Amen.

The Litany of Loretto

(originally approved in 1587 by Pope Sixtus V)

Lord, have mercy.
Christ, have mercy.
Lord, have mercy.
Christ, hear us.
Christ, graciously hear us.
God, the Father of heaven,
have mercy on us.
God the Son, Redeemer of the world,
have mercy on us.
God the Holy Spirit,
have mercy on us.
Holy Trinity, one God.
have mercy on us.
Holy Mary, *pray for us.**
Holy Mother of God,
Holy Virgin of virgins,
Mother of Christ,
Mother of the Church,
Mother of divine grace,

**Pray for us* is repeated after each invocation.

102

Mother most pure,
Mother most chaste,
Mother inviolate,
Mother undefiled,
Mother most amiable,
Mother most admirable,
Mother of good counsel,
Mother of our Creator,
Mother of our Savior,
Virgin most prudent,
Virgin most venerable,
Virgin most renowned,
Virgin most powerful,
Virgin most merciful,
Virgin most faithful,
Mirror of justice,
Seat of wisdom,
Cause of our joy,
Spiritual vessel,
Vessel of honor,
Singular vessel of devotion,
Mystical rose,
Tower of David,
Tower of ivory,
House of gold,
Ark of the covenant,
Gate of heaven,
Morning star,
Health of the sick,
Refuge of sinners,
Comforter of the afflicted,
Help of Christians,
Queen of angels,
Queen of patriarchs,
Queen of prophets,

Queen of apostles,
Queen of martyrs,
Queen of confessors,
Queen of virgins,
Queen of all saints,
Queen conceived without original sin,
Queen assumed into heaven,
Queen of the most holy Rosary,
Queen of families
Queen of peace.
Lamb of God, You take away sins of the world;
spare us, O Lord.
Lamb of God, You take away the sins of the world;
Graciously hear us, O Lord.
Lamb of God, Your take away the sins of the world;
have mercy on us.

V. Pray for us, O Holy Mother of God.
R. *That we may be made worthy of the promises of Christ.*

Let us pray.

Grant, we beg you, O Lord God, that we your servants may enjoy lasting health of mind and body, and by the glorious intercession of the Blessed Mary, ever Virgin, be delivered from present sorrow and enter into the joy of eternal happiness. Through Christ Our Lord.

R. Amen.

Mary, Help of Those in Need

Holy Mary, help those in need, give strength to the weak, comfort the sorrowful, pray for God's people, assist the clergy, intercede for religious. Mary, all who seek your help experience your unfailing protection.
Amen.

Hail, You Star of Ocean

Hail, you Star of Ocean! Portal of the sky, ever Virgin Mother, of the Lord most high. O! by Gabriel's Ave, uttered long ago, Eve's name reversing, establish peace below. Break the captive's fetters; light on blindness pour; All our ills expelling, ev'ry bliss implore. Show yourself a mother; offer Him our sighs, Who for us Incarnate did not you despise. Virgin of all virgins! To your shelter take us; gentlest of the gentle! Chaste and gentle make us. Still as on we journey, help our weak endeavor, till with you and Jesus we rejoice forever. Through the highest heaven, To the Almighty Three, Father, Son, and Spirit, One same glory be.

(Note: The Latin version of this prayer, Ave, Maris Stella, can be traced to the late eighth/early ninth century. The title, Star of the Sea, is one of the oldest and most cherished titles for Mary. The prayer is often used to pray for travelers. Mary herself is a sign of hope for a safe arrival to one's destination.)

"Lord, may the prayers of the Virgin Mary bring us protection from danger and freedom from sin that we may come to the joy of Your peace."

**— From the Common of
the Blessed Virgin Mary**

105

Holy Mary, Mother of God

"If our faith is weak, we should turn to Mary. St. John tells us that it was because of the miracle that Christ performed, at His mother's request, at the marriage feast at Cana, that 'His disciples learned to believe in Him.' Our mother is always interceding with her Son, so that He may attend to our needs and show Himself to us in such a way that we can cry out, 'You are the Son of God.' "

— Blessed Josémaria Escrivá

"The Blessed Mother of Christ . . . shows herself a mother also by her care and loving attention. For her heart is not hardened against these children as if they were not her own; her womb carried a child only once, yet it remains ever fruitful, never ceasing to bring forth the fruits of motherly compassion."

— St. Guerric of Igny

"It is because (Mary) is, of all the saints, the most perfectly poor and the most perfectly hidden, the one who has absolutely nothing whatever that she attempts to possess as her own, that she can most fully communicate to the rest of us the grace of the infinitely selfless God. And we will most truly possess Him when we have emptied ourselves and become poor and hidden as she is, resembling Him by resembling her. And all our sanctity depends on her maternal love. The ones she desires to share the joy of her own poverty and simplicity, the ones whom she wills to be hidden as she is hidden, are the ones who share her closeness to God."

— Thomas Merton

How to Pray the Rosary

One of the most unmistakeably Catholic items is the rosary — the set of beads on which millions of people offer prayer with Mary each day. The Rosary is an ideal Marian prayer because, as with all the works of Mary, it serves to draw us closer to her divine Son, Jesus. The Rosary is an ancient prayer, which took its present form in the Middle Ages.

When people say the word "Rosary," they can be referring to one of two things: either the set of beads used to count out Marian prayers, or the prayers themselves. A rosary is a set of beads that follow a pattern: one bead by itself, followed by ten beads grouped together. On the stand-alone bead, we pray an Our Father. On each of the ten beads, we pray a Hail Mary. The sets of ten beads are called "decades," and there are five decades in an ordinary rosary. (There are other variations on the beads, including ring rosaries, which can be worn on one's finger, and pocket rosaries, which are one decade long.)

"No enemy on earth fears a powerful hostile army as much as the demons of hell fear the name and protection of Mary."

— St. Bonaventure

The term "Rosary" also refers to the set of prayers and meditations that we count on the strung beads. We *can* say the prayers of the Rosary without using beads. But the action of moving one's fingers along the beads is beneficial because it takes yet another of our senses up into our prayer, and the beads do make it easier for us to count the prayers.

Normally one begins the Rosary by reciting the Apostles' Creed while holding the crucifix of the Rosary. After the cross comes one individual bead followed by three consecutive beads. As the fingers take up that first solitary bead, we recite an Our Father. On each of the three consecutive beads, we say a Hail Mary; it is customary to offer these three prayers for an increase of faith, hope, and charity. Next we say a Glory Be before moving to the next individual bead. This forms the introductory prayer to the traditional five-decade Rosary.

With each decade, then, we meditate on one of the events, or "mysteries," in the life of Jesus and Mary. Before beginning each decade, we call to mind that event. There are fifteen of these particular mysteries, and they are divided into three sets of five: the Joyful, Sorrowful, and Glorious Mysteries. The Joyful Mysteries recall the events surrounding the conception, birth, and childhood of Jesus. The Sorrowful Mysteries focus on His suffering and death. The Glorious Mysteries begin with Jesus' resurrection and move on to heavenly realities. All fifteen mysteries together comprise an entire Rosary. Usually only five are covered in each recitation.

After recalling one of the mysteries, we say an Our

Father while holding the stand-alone bead. Then we move along the ten consecutive beads, praying a Hail Mary with each one. We conclude each decade with a Glory Be. Then we continue with another mystery and repeat the process until we've completed five decades.

Some people follow each decade's Glory Be with a "Fatima Prayer" (found on page 114), a short prayer that the Blessed Mother taught to three little children in Portugal in 1917. Another pious custom is to end the recitation of the Rosary by praying the Hail Holy Queen, another ancient prayer, in honor of the Blessed Mother.

Try to pray the Rosary in an unhurried manner with a quiet rhythm. Take time after announcing the particular mystery to orient your meditation before beginning the recitation of the decade.

Hold That Thought

The Rosary is best prayed when the mind is free to contemplate the mysteries. The best time is when you have fifteen minutes or so to devote entirely to the prayer. But you can also pray the Rosary fruitfully during physical activity that does not monopolize your thoughts — such as mowing the lawn, doing the dishes, or driving the car.

Pray the Rosary daily. If you can't find the time just now, start with just one decade per day. The habit allows you to grow in the prayer and over time, it engraves the truths of the fifteen mysteries upon your heart and mind.

The Rosary is an ideal prayer for family devotion It provides a format that children can learn quickly. It also allows older children to have the opportunity to lead prayers. In the family Rosary or in group recitation, the leader prays the first half of each prayer (Our Father . . . Hail Mary . . . Glory Be . . .) while the rest of the group recites the second half (Give us this day . . . Holy Mary . . . As it was in the beginning . . .).

The Rosary is also a profoundly biblical prayer. Reading a scriptural quotation or some other meditation that pertains to the particular mystery can enhance our understanding. There are many good collections of Rosary meditations and Scripture verses.

October is the month of the Rosary and provides an excellent opportunity for an individual or family to grow in this devotion.

The Fifteen Mysteries
of the Rosary

The Joyful Mysteries:

(Used on Mondays and Thursdays, and the Sundays from the First Sunday of Advent until Lent.)

1. The Annunciation
2. The Visitation
3. The Birth of Our Lord Jesus Christ
4. The Presentation at the Temple
5. The Finding at the Temple

The Sorrowful Mysteries:

(Used on Tuesdays and Fridays, and the Sundays of Lent.)

1. The Agony of Christ in the Garden
2. The Scourging at the Pillar
3. The Crowning with Thorns
4. The Carrying of the Cross
5. The Crucifixion and Death of Our Lord

Glorious Mysteries:

(Used on Wednesdays and Saturdays, and the Sundays from Easter until Advent.)

1. The Resurrection of Our Lord
2. The Ascension of Our Lord
3. The Coming of the Holy Spirit upon the Apostles
4. The Assumption of the Virgin Mary
5. The Coronation of the Virgin Mary

Prayers of the Rosary

The Apostles' Creed

I believe in God, the Father Almighty, Creator of Heaven and earth. I believe in Jesus Christ, His only Son, Our Lord. He was conceived by the power of the Holy Spirit and was born of the Virgin Mary. He suffered under Pontius Pilate, was crucified, died, and was buried. He descended to the dead. On the third day He rose again. He ascended into Heaven, and is seated at the right hand of the Father. He will come again to judge the living and the dead. I believe in the Holy Spirit, the Holy Catholic Church, the Communion of Saints, the forgiveness of sins, the resurrection of the body, and life everlasting. Amen.

Our Father

Our Father, Who art in Heaven; hallowed be Thy name; Thy kingdom come; Thy will be done on earth as it is in Heaven. Give us this day our daily bread; and forgive us our trespasses as we forgive those who trespass against us, and lead us not into temptation; but deliver us from evil. Amen.

Hail Mary

Hail Mary, full of grace, the Lord is with thee; blessed art thou among women, and blessed is the fruit of thy womb, Jesus. Holy Mary, Mother of God, pray for us sinners, now and at the hour of our death. Amen.

Glory Be

Glory be to the Father, and to the Son, and to the Holy Spirit, as it was in the beginning, is now, and ever shall be, world without end. Amen.

Praying the Rosary

1. After making the Sign of the Cross, say the Apostles' Creed.

2. Say the Our Father.

3. Say three Hail Marys.

4. Say the Glory Be.

5. Announce the first mystery, then say the Our Father.

6. Read the first Scripture excerpt, then say the first Hail Mary while meditating on the mystery.

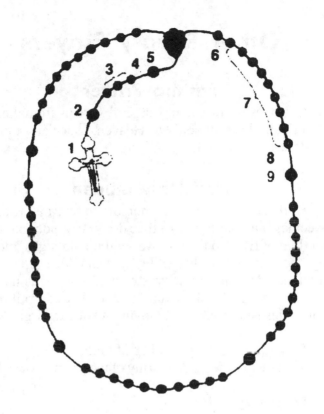

7. Repeat step 6 for the nine remaining Hail Marys in the decade.

8. Say the Glory Be.

9. Announce the second mystery, then say the Our Father. Repeat steps 6, 7, and 8 and continue with the third, fourth, and fifth mysteries in the same manner.

10. While not essential, it is very fitting to say the Hail Holy Queen at the end of the Rosary, then kiss the cross and make the Sign of the Cross.

Other Rosary Prayers

Fatima Prayer

O my Jesus, forgive us our sins, save us from the fires of hell, and lead all souls to Heaven, especially those in most need of Your Mercy. Amen.

Hail Holy Queen

Hail, Holy Queen, Mother of mercy, our life, our sweetness and our hope. To thee do we cry, poor banished children of Eve. To thee do we send up our sighs, mourning and weeping in this valley of tears. Turn then, most gracious advocate, thine eyes of mercy towards us. And after this our exile, show unto us the blessed Fruit of thy womb, Jesus. O clement, O loving, O sweet Virgin Mary.

Pray for us, O holy Mother of God.
That we may be made worthy of the promises of Christ.

Let us pray:

O God, Whose only-begotten Son, by His life, death, and resurrection, has purchased for us the rewards of eternal life, grant, we beseech You, that meditating upon these Mysteries of the Holy Rosary of the Blessed Virgin Mary, we may imitate what they contain, and obtain what they promise, through the same Christ, Our Lord. Amen.

A Wreath of Roses

"The Rosary is my favorite prayer. A marvelous prayer. Marvelous in its simplicity and depth . . . I cordially exhort everyone to recite it."

— **Pope John Paul II**

"The Rosary will be your little wreath of roses, your crown for Jesus and Mary."

— **St. Louis de Montfort**

"Therefore let all men, the learned and the ignorant, the just and the sinner, the great and the small praise and honor Jesus and Mary night and day by saying the Most Holy Rosary."

— **St. Louis de Montfort**

How to Pray the Angelus and Other Noonday Prayers

Parents and teachers often remind young children to eat their lunch. They're right, of course. Halfway through the day, it makes sense to stop and take some nourishment — to give us the strength we need for the rest of the day.

Spiritual masters, for their part, recommend that we take a moment in the early afternoon to recollect ourselves before God. It gives us an opportunity to renew the offering we made in the morning, refocus our attention, and acknowledge that God is with us. There's no better way to regain strength for the second half of the day.

This time of prayer need not be long, perhaps five minutes. If you've read Scripture in the morning, or if you jotted something down after your morning prayer, noon is your chance to recall that thought to mind. Some people also use midday as the time to examine their conscience, turning over in their mind the day's events so far.

There is also a formal prayer that is customary at noon. This prayer is the Angelus or the Regina Caeli, depending on the season of the year. The Angelus commemorates the mystery of the incarnation of the eternal Word in the womb of the Virgin Mary. In the prayers of the Angelus, we also ask the intercession of the Blessed Mother. The alternating scriptural phrases can be recited by two or more people as a public prayer. An individual will privately recite the phrases. Punctuated with three Hail Marys, the Angelus provides an opportunity to meditate on the mystery of salvation and give thanks. A prayer for the grace of final perseverance ends this midday prayer.

During the Easter Season (from Easter Sunday to Pentecost), another prayer, the Regina Caeli, replaces the Angelus. This prayer celebrates the resurrection.

Prayers

The Angelus

Leader: The Angel of the Lord announced unto Mary.
Response: And she conceived by the Holy Spirit.
Hail Mary. . .
Leader: Behold the handmaid of the Lord.
Response: Be it done unto me according to Thy word.
Hail Mary. . .
Leader: And the Word was made flesh.
Response: And dwelt among us.
Hail Mary. . .

Leader: Let us pray. Pour forth, we beg Thee, O Lord, Thy grace into our hearts: that we to whom the Incarnation of Christ Thy Son was made known by the message of an Angel, may by His Passion and cross be brought to the glory of His resurrection. Through the same Christ Our Lord. Amen.

Regina Caeli

Queen of Heaven, rejoice, *Alleluia,*
For He Whom You did merit to bear, *Alleluia,*
Has risen as He said, *Alleluia,*
Pray to God for us, *Alleluia,*
Rejoice and be glad, O Virgin Mary, *Alleluia,*
The Lord has truly risen, *Alleluia.*

Let us pray. O God, Who gave joy to the world through the resurrection of Your Son, Our Lord Jesus Christ: grant, we beg You, that through the intercession of the Virgin Mary, His Mother, we may lay hold of the joys of eternal life. Through the same Christ Our Lord. Amen.

Consider This

We tend to be very busy, keeping a frenetic pace at work, in our social life, and even in our leisure. It is easy to become so involved in our workday that we lose sight of the fact that God is with us. Our noontime prayer can be like taking a breath of fresh air. It allows us to reestablish our priorities and acknowledge Jesus as Our Lord. Noon is a natural time, too, to take a break. If a lunch bell doesn't remind you to say the Angelus, perhaps your growling stomach will.

What we do reflects our priorities. One woman told us she often forgets to pray the Angelus, though she never forgets to watch her favorite television show, which, coincidentally, begins at noon. Recognition of such a shortcoming can be the first step on our way to reclaiming our day for Christ.

Penitential Devotions

How to Examine Your Conscience

Sometimes it takes a pagan to sum up a Christian truth. Socrates, four hundred years before Christ, declared that "the unexamined life is not worth living." Our everyday experience bears him out. How often we find ourselves in need of a "reality check" — time to stand back and see things as they really are, and not as we've made them out to be.

Well, God wants even more than that. He wants us to see our days as He sees them — and we can't do that without a regular examination of conscience. Simply defined, "the exam" is a review of the day's events, measuring each thought, word, and deed against the moral law and the demands of the Christian vocation.

The unexamined life is not worth living because it cannot lead us to heaven. The prophet Jeremiah exhorted Israel: "Let us search and examine our ways, that we may return to the LORD" (Lam 3:40 NAB). In the New Testament, St. Paul insisted (1 Cor 11:28-31 NAB) that "a man

119

should examine himself" before receiving Holy Communion. The apostle goes on to say that laxity in self-examination was leading people to receive Jesus unworthily: "That is why many among you are sick and infirm, and a considerable number are dying" (1 Cor 12:30).

Christians have always known that St. Paul wasn't exaggerating. In the centuries that followed, they developed a more formal spiritual discipline for examination of conscience.

St. Ignatius of Loyola, founder of the Jesuits, usually gets the credit for dividing the exam into two parts: the general examination and the particular examination. The general exam is a thorough review of the day; it aims at the correction of all sorts of faults. The particular exam focuses instead on the avoidance of one specific fault or the acquisition of one specific virtue. In the general exam, we might say, the soul does damage control. In the particular exam, the soul makes a concentrated effort to advance.

What's the best thing to work on? That's up to the individual soul, consulting with a good spiritual director or confessor. But it should be something very specific, and thus more measurable. It should be challenging, but doable, thus avoiding the dangers of both pride and despair.

St. Ignatius urges us to have our particular struggle in mind on rising out of bed in the morning. About noon, then, we should consider how we're doing. Finally, at night, we should see how we've done in our particular struggle throughout the day, and we should make a resolution for the next day.

In the general exam, most people prefer to move chronologically through the day, sometimes with their appointment calendar nearby to jog the memory. It's good to acknowledge our sins as soon as we recognize them, promise to try to do better, and then move on without delay.

It's never good to dwell overmuch on individual actions. For further clarification we can, eventually, consult a confessor. But at the time of the exam, it's best just to say we're sorry and leave the ultimate examination to God, because that's where it rests, anyway.

The examination is a gift. It's our one chance, each day, to see things as they really are — and not as we dress them up for the boss or the spouse. It's when we see our life in the light of the Eternal Day.

An Examination of Conscience

1. In the morning, as soon as you wake up, make up your mind to watch most carefully lest you fall into that particular defect which you wish to correct.

2. During the day, when you notice that you have erred, at once with some interior prayer . . . ask God for His forgiveness; with your hand on your heart, promise to be more attentive in the future.

3. In the evening when you make your general examination, after having made a general survey of all your faults, give particular attention to this one.

4. Compare the second day with the first, the third with the second . . . and so on. In this way, you will know whether or not you are progressing in virtue, and whether you are getting any good out of the particular examination.

5. You may also make some virtue the subject of the particular examination. Those who make the particular and general examination in the evening when they go to bed, as well as during the day, redouble their speed and in a short time make further progress along the road of virtue.

—Pope John XXIII

Examination of Conscience

(Some Suggested Questions)

Do I pray to God every day? Do I pray for my family and friends?

Have I thanked God for His gifts to me?

Am I attentive at Mass? Do I receive Communion with care and attention?

Have I worked unnecessarily on Sunday?

Have I missed attending Mass on Sundays or holy days of obligation?

Have I spoken God's name in disrespectful ways?

Have I respected and obeyed my elders, parents, employers, or teachers?

Have I physically harmed other people through acts of violence or neglect?

Have I committed any acts of violence?

Have I respected God's laws and the Church's laws concerning marriage?

Have I committed adultery?

Outside of marriage, have I shown another person affection in ways appropriate only between a husband and wife?

In marriage am I open to having any children God may send?

Have I used artificial birth control to prevent God's creation of new life?

Have I taken anything that I had no right to take?

Have I pilfered office supplies or items belonging to my employer?

Have I shared all that I should — of my belongings, my time, my friendship?

Have I treated other people's property carelessly?

Have I said things that I knew would hurt someone?

Have I gossiped?

Have I lied?

Have I emphasized the negative qualities of other people or their work?

Have I spoken badly of the Church?

Have I boasted about myself or my work?

Have I been dishonest — with my employer, my family, the tax officials, or anyone else?

Have I placed false information on forms or in reports at work or at school? Is there anyone I have made to feel unwelcome in my presence?

In my thoughts or glances, have I invaded anyone's privacy in a way that would make them hurt or uncomfortable if they knew?

Have I used well the time and talents God has given me?

Have I offered my co-workers, friends, and family a good example of Christian life? Do I speak to them about God, and offer to pray with them or for them?

Are there people I have refused to forgive?

Do I dress modestly?

Have I envied other people for the things they own or the friends they have?

Have I allowed the desire for a better home or car, clothing or vacation, appliances or other material goods to disturb my inner peace?

Have I used another person for my own pleasure, convenience, or advancement?

Do I tell people how much I appreciate them?

How to Go to Confession

(Sacrament of Reconciliation and Penance)

Many people miss out on confession, not because they don't know how to go — but because they're afraid or they're lacking in self-knowledge. So any instruction on the Sacrament of Penance should begin with practical advice on overcoming these obstacles.

It's natural, perhaps, to fear confession if you don't go to the sacrament very often. The sheer number of your sins, accumulated over many months or even years, can seem staggering. Maybe you feel ashamed, too, of the sins you've committed, and you dread speaking them aloud. Maybe you're afraid of looking someone in the face as you tell your sins.

But the best cure for this fear is just to dive right in. Make your appointment, examine your conscience, and go. It's best to be frank with the priest. If you feel uncomfortable looking at him while you confess, you should tell him that, too, and ask if he might hear your confession from behind a screen, which is a traditional option for the sacrament. Sometimes, however — as at a parish penance service — face-to-face confession is the only possibility. In such circumstances, we can offer this humiliation to God as a more demanding penance, to "make up" for our sins. Or we can resolve to call a priest immediately on returning home, in order to schedule a more relaxed confession.

In any event, once you've begun your confession, you should do the best you can in telling your sins, asking the priest for guidance whenever you need it. If you're worried that shame will hang you up, then start off by telling him the sin that shames you most. Doing this produces a remarkable sense of relief that can last for the rest of your confession. Holding back, on the other hand, just makes your anxiety grow.

Rest assured that the fear of confession tends to disappear if you make a habit of the sacrament. If you're going at least once a month (twice a month is better) to a priest you've chosen as your regular confessor, you'll grow accustomed to opening your soul to him.

If you avoid penance because you don't think your sins are serious enough, then you probably need to deepen your self-knowledge and your knowledge of God. (See the chapter on "How to Examine Your Conscience.") The Bible tells us: "If we say, 'We are without sin,' we deceive ourselves, and the truth is not in us" (1 Jn 1:8 NAB). The sacrament itself will help us on our way to self-knowledge. For there is a world of difference between thinking about our sins and speaking about them to another person. When we speak our faults aloud, God helps us confront them in a powerful way.

Confession is the ordinary way that Jesus gave us to reconcile ourselves with God and with the Church. He gave His first priests the power to forgive sins in His name (Jn 20:23), and His priests continue this ministry today. In the sacrament, God Himself forgives us; the priest, acting in the person of Christ, dispenses God's healing with the words of absolution: "I absolve you. . . ."

The Sacrament of Reconciliation follows a certain form, yet its structure provides both you and the priest more flexibility than do other sacramental rituals, like the Mass. Still, there are certain elements of a good confession, and you can consider them in three phases: preparation for confession, the actual time of confession, and after confession.

BEFORE YOU GO . . . you should make a thorough examination of conscience. If you have practiced a regular, daily examination, you will be well aware of your most troublesome sins and failings. Still, a time of more thorough reflection is appropriate before confession. Again, you can use the commandments or the beatitudes, or questions such as the ones on pages 122 and 123, to help you prepare.

Next, you need to be sincerely sorry for your sins. This can take some work, since often our sins bring us pleasure. Yet you should tell Our Lord, at least, that you want to be sorry for your sins, and you want to receive His forgiveness and grow in love and obedience. You should also make a firm purpose of amendment — promising God that you will do all you can, with His help, to avoid such sins in the future.

WHEN YOU GO . . . Then comes the actual time of confession — the Rite of Reconciliation. After the customary greetings, you make the Sign of the Cross, saying: "In the name of the Father, and of the Son, and of the Holy Spirit."

The priest will likely urge you to have confidence in God. He may say: "May the Lord be in your heart and on your lips that you may confess your sins with sorrow."

You may then briefly tells the priest your state in life and the time passed since your last confession. For example: "Bless me, Father, for I have sinned. It has been three weeks since my last confession. I am married with children."

Then tell your sins and the number of times you've committed each. In order for the sacrament to be valid, you must confess any mortal (or grave) sins you have committed. If, to your knowledge, you have committed no mortal sins, then confess the venial sins you've committed since your last confession. When you've finished, you may conclude with these or similar words: "For these and for all the sins of my past life, I am truly sorry."

The priest may give advice or ask you to clarify some matter before assigning your "penance" — some prayer or good work that you must offer to God in reparation for your sins. He will then ask you to make an Act of Contrition. You may use your own words or a traditional Act of Contrition. One example is: "Lord Jesus, Son of God, have mercy on me, a sinner."

NEXT . . . THE PRIEST WILL GIVE YOU ABSOLUTION: "God, the Father of mercies, through the death and resurrection of His Son, has reconciled the world to Himself and sent His Holy Spirit among us for the forgiveness of sins; through the ministry of the Church, may God give you pardon and peace, and I absolve you from your sins in the name of the Father, and of the Son, and of the Holy Spirit."

And you answer: "Amen."

The priest dismisses you with this prayer or one like it:

"May the Passion of Our Lord Jesus Christ, the intercession of the Blessed Virgin Mary and of all the saints, whatever good you do and suffering you endure heal your sins, help you to grow in holiness, and reward you with eternal life. Go in peace."

After the completion of the rite, you should fulfill your assigned penance as soon as possible.

Hold That Thought

Be clear in what you say in confession. Don't sentimentalize or try to be subtle. When you examined your conscience, you formed in your mind the matter of the sin. Tell it directly to the priest without embellishment.

Yet there is no need to go into great detail. Often, spending time in details is just a way for us to excuse ourselves or minimize our guilt. So be brief.

What happens if you forget a sin? If you inadvertently forget something serious, don't worry, but tell God you're sorry immediately, and return to confession as soon as you can.

How often should you go to confession? That depends. If you commit a serious (mortal) sin, you need to receive sacramental absolution in confession as soon as possible — and you must confess your mortal sin before you can receive Communion again. If you do not have serious sin to confess, you technically do not have to go to confession, though the Church does encourage us to go at least once a year. This is sometimes considered part of a Catholic's "Easter duty" — the obligation to receive Holy Communion during the Easter season, confession being a necessary prerequisite to our reception of Communion if we are in sin.

But we need to remind ourselves of our goal: we want our relationship with Christ to grow. We want to fall more deeply in love, and we know that lovers never want to offend their beloved. We don't want our faults, whether great or small, to hinder our relationship. In confession, we make certain that our relationship with Christ continues to grow and that all impediments are removed. Most spiritual writers recommend confession at least monthly.

Forgive me . . .

"The highest motive for purging out all affection for sin is a strong, living conviction of the great evils sins bring upon us. In this way we arrive at a deep, intense contrition."

— **St. Francis de Sales**

"Why should the sinner be ashamed to make known his sins, since they are already known and manifest to God, and to His angels, and even to the blessed in heaven? Confession opens the door to heaven. Confession brings hope of salvation. Because of this the Scripture says: 'First, tell thy iniquities, that you may be justified' (Is 43:26). Here we are shown that the man will not be saved who, during his life does not confess his sins. Neither will that confession deliver you which is made without true repentance. For true repentance is grief of heart and sorrow of soul because of the evils a man has committed. True repentance causes us to grieve over them with a firm intention of never committing them again."

— **St. Ambrose**

"Can one forgive the offense committed against another? No; yet the priest says: 'I absolve thee.' How can he say it? Because it is Christ Who says it by His mouth."

— **Dom Columba Marmion**

How to Choose a Confessor

Some people worry about the priest to whom they confess. It's a legitimate concern. Not that the grace we receive depends upon the virtue or wisdom of the priest. It doesn't. *Any priest*, by the grace of his state in life, will suffice for our forgiveness, since he is pronouncing absolution with the power of Jesus Christ. That power more than makes up for any of Father's deficiencies.

There is, however, great benefit in finding a regular confessor who can get to know you and advise you on the particular circumstances of your life. A confessor who sees us regularly will, over time, come to see our habits of sin — and see them better than we do. Thus equipped, he can watch for patterns of temptation and help us, perhaps, to trace our common sins back to a single dominant fault. Then he can help us to concentrate on overcoming that fault.

But how do you find that outstanding priest — wise, holy, faithful, merciful, and available? Try following these steps:

• First, pray about it. Ask the Holy Spirit to show you the way to a good confessor.

• Next, be clear about what you're looking for. Make a list of qualities you think you'd find in a good confessor.

• If you have special needs or struggles, check with others who are in the same situation. Immigrants may benefit from a priest who speaks their language or understands their culture. Alcoholics, people with mental illness, or those who are coping with an abusive past all can benefit from specialized care in the confessional. Tap into networks and support groups for leads. Or call the clergy office in your chancery.

• Some Catholic professional groups also have chaplains who specialize in their particular circumstances. Firefighters, police, doctors, and lawyers are a few examples. Again, your diocesan clergy office can provide you with information.

• Then start looking in your own parish. The priests there have a special "grace of state" to serve their parishioners.

• Listen to the homilies of each "candidate." Are they substantial and clear? Do they show fidelity to Church teaching? Does Father seem to be a man of charity and prayer?

• You might set an appointment to speak with Father in greater detail and get a better sense of his compatibility with you.

• If you don't find Father Right in your parish, call around to local retreat houses, monasteries, or religious orders. Ask them to recommend some candidates who live near you.

• Then, if you think you've found a priest who will challenge you, guide you, and show you the mercy you need, go to him for confession. After one or two visits, you'll know for sure whether you want to stay with him for the long haul.

Act of Contrition

O my God, I am heartily sorry for having offended You and I detest all my sins, because I dread the loss of heaven and the pains of hell; but most of all because they offend You, my God, Who are all good and deserving of all my love. I firmly resolve with the help of Your grace, to confess my sins, to do penance, and to amend my life. Amen.

How to "Offer It Up"

"Offer it up!" More than one Catholic parent has said these words to a complaining child. It's an idea that has been with the Church since the New Testament. It is also called sacrifice, self-denial, or mortification.

"Though [Jesus] was in the form of God, [He] did not count equality with God a thing to be grasped, but emptied Himself, taking the form of a servant, being born in the likeness of men. And being found in human form He humbled Himself and became obedient unto death, even death on a cross" (Phil 2:6-8). Our understanding of sacrifice and mortification comes from Christ. He "offered up" His position in the Godhead and became a man. The creator of the universe humbled Himself to be born of a woman. The Lord of all allowed Himself to be judged by a Roman bureaucrat. The Life of the world died on the cross. Now, that's sacrifice!

We can imitate Christ by our own sacrifices. In fact, He has commanded us to take up our cross *every day*. Well, we never have to look far for the cross. In this world, we daily encounter difficulty, pain, suffering, discomfort, illness, delays, annoyances, interruptions, or disappointments. These are inevitable. But how we handle them is a matter of free will. We can grumble and complain, or we can join our difficulties to the suffering of Christ. If we choose to "offer it up" with Jesus, our suffering, discomfort, or struggle can become redemptive for ourselves and for others.

For our sake, Christ presented His body as a living sacrifice to the Father — the only sacrifice that was worthy of God. When we join our own sacrifices with His, they rise like incense before the throne of the Father. Read what St. Paul said to the Colossians (1:24): Christ wants us to make up in our own bodies what is lacking in His

> "A true sacrifice is any work done that we may cleave to God in holy fellowship."
>
> — **St. Augustine**

suffering, for the sake of our neighbors, co-workers, and family members.

When we're delayed in traffic, we can offer our impatience for young singles we know who have to wait patiently to find a spouse. When we are served food we don't really like, we can offer our displeasure for the sake of someone who's facing a much more unpleasant situation in life. Thus, none of our suffering, great or small, is ever meaningless or useless.

How do we accomplish this type of prayer? We accept trials and difficulties as part of God's will for us, trusting that Christ "works for good with those who love Him, who are called according to His purpose" (Rom 8:28). When we embrace this approach, our lives can become better conformed to the will of God.

An example: A co-worker regularly speaks negatively about you to others. Instead of allowing anger and resentment to control you, you pray: "Lord, You suffered far worse out of love for me. Out of love for You, Lord, I accept this trial and join it to Your trials. I pray that this situation may ultimately be for Your glory."

And there's nothing wrong with offering mortification for our own benefit — so that we grow in virtue, make a good confession, find the job or the friendship we desire. We will find, in the long run, that mortification benefits us anyway. Keep in mind what the athletic trainers say: no pain, no gain. When we "offer it up," the pain we accept makes us stronger, more courageous, more willing and able to endure (Rom 9:24-27).

So far we've spoken about difficulties that are beyond our control. But "offering it up" works also for sacrifices that we choose for ourselves. For example, you can by-pass a dessert with a silent prayer that God will bless your spouse. Or you might sacrifice some sleep, rising earlier in the morning and offering it for the sake of a friend. These small, seemingly inconsequential decision take on tremendous meaning when they are joined to the work of Christ.

Of course, we should *never* overdo our sacrifices, bring harm upon ourselves, or hinder our ability to fulfill our duties. Mortifications are best moderated in conversation with a confessor, spiritual director, or mature Catholic friend. Some saints were called to great sacrifices for the Gospel. Most of us, however, are not called to volunteer such severe mortifications; to grasp after them could lead us to sinful pride or lack of charity for ourselves.

Still, this is an area where most of us could stand to grow. One way to begin is to identify the irritants that already exist in your life, stop grumbling, and start praying.

Hold That Thought

Any spiritual devotion is subject to misuse and mis-understanding. This devotion is no exception. Our goal is to make sure that Jesus is Lord of every aspect of our lives, and that we are consciously living that reality. If we find that sleep is lord of our lives at precisely the time we're supposed to be waking up, we can and should willingly deny ourselves — and get out of bed. The Church has always recommended fasting and abstinence as forms of sacrifice and mortification.

"By sacrifice man acknowledges God as the author of his being and as the unique source of his beatitude."

— **Edward Leen**

Offer It Up

"The value of mortification is as a means to an end; it is the end that interprets and sanctifies the means. And this end is not death but life. It is not the act of mortification itself nor the pain it costs which gives it its value, but what it gains. It is not the mere giving up but the receiving, the surrender of something good in itself for something better."

— Father B.W. Maturin

"Mortification . . . is not performed in a morbid sense of self-hatred or contempt of the body; it is not a mere negative thing, a foolish frustration or self repression. It is something quite positive; an 'assertion' of Jesus rather than a denial of self; for we only deny ourselves to find Him, that He may live in us and that we may be united to Him."

— Dom Eugene Boylan

"Care in little things requires constant mortification. It is a way to make life more agreeable for others."

— Blessed Josémaria Escrivá

How to Fast

No, it's not a Christian weight-loss program. Fasting is among the most powerful and time-honored Christian forms of prayer. Jesus said that fasting accomplishes what other prayers cannot. The apostles fasted whenever they faced an important event.

To fast is to limit the intake of food and drink for a religious purpose.

Fasting is to prayer what an exclamation point is to a sentence. It adds a sense of urgency. Fasting often accompanied prayer in both the Old and New Testament. When Israel faced a strong army (Jgs 20) and when national disaster loomed on the horizon (Est 4), the people fasted and prayed. The apostles fasted and prayed before they sent Paul and Barnabas on their missionary work. Jesus prayed and fasted for forty days in the desert before He began His public ministry.

Food and water are created by God and necessary for human life. Yet we need more than these. We need to fill ourselves with God. To fast is to deny ourselves something good in order to focus on something better. In our prayer, we give our petitions to God with the knowledge that it is He whom we really need. He is our strength and sufficiency. When we fast, we embody that prayer in an action. Our physical hunger helps us to bring clarity — only God is the answer to our needs. We are dependent upon Him. Fasting can also can help us to listen in prayer.

Fasting is often associated with penance. The Book of Leviticus prescribes fasting as a part of seeking atonement for sins. When we sin, we choose some worldly pleasure over God and His law. When we fast, we do the opposite: we renounce a worldly good and pleasure in order to give ourselves more completely to God.

As with other forms of sacrifice and mortification,

we can use fasting as part of our prayer for others. We ask God to bless and minister to our neighbor, and our fasting emphasizes our prayer and commitment to our neighbor. Also, the physical hunger reminds us of our commitment to prayer.

The Church has always emphasized the importance of fasting. One of the six precepts (commandments) of the Church states: "You shall observe the prescribed days of fasting and abstinence." At present in the United States, a Catholic is required to fast on Ash Wednesday and Good Friday. That means, we must limit food intake to one full meal and two smaller meals that, taken together, do not equal a full meal. (If health or age require a greater intake of food, the requirement to fast from food is dispensed. Some other form of penance can be substituted.) Abstinence from meat is also required on these two days as well on all Fridays during Lent. These are the minimal requirements. We should examine ourselves on how we might go beyond the minimum to love God and neighbor through the practice of fasting.

Consider This

In Matthew 6:16 Jesus teaches "When you fast, do not look dismal, like the hypocrites." There are a couple of items we should notice in this passage. First there is a presumption that we *will* fast. It is not *if* we fast, but *when* we fast. Jesus also points out that there is an incorrect way to fast.

If your fasting makes you grumpy and unbearable to live with, then something is wrong. Jesus tells His disciples that no one should know they are fasting except "your Father Who is in secret; and your Father Who sees in secret will reward you" (Mt 6:18).

Also, fasting needs to be in proper balance with the other aspects of your Christian life. Many spiritual writers point out that prayer and almsgiving must accompany fasting, if fasting is to have the desired effect.

It is helpful to make fasting a regular part of your spiritual game plan. Friday is the traditional day for fasting, since it is on that day that we focus on the crucifixion of the Lord. The amount of fasting can vary. Some may wish to follow the fast that is now required on Ash Wednesday and Good Friday. Others may wish to do more, perhaps only eating one meal during the day. Others may want to take the approach of abstinence from a specific food or food group. For example, no meat or no dessert on certain days.

Any serious fasts that would extend more than a day or two consecutively should be undertaken only after conferring with a priest.

More Than Bread and Water

"Let not anyone listen to the tempter inwardly suggesting such things as these: 'What do you do that prompts you to fast? You are cheating your soul; you are not giving it what pleases it; you are imposing punishment upon yourself; you are your own torturer and executioner. Does it please God to have you torment yourself? Then He is cruel, since He is pleased by your suffering.' Answer a tempter of this sort with these words: 'Certainly I punish myself so that He may spare me; I take vengeance on myself so that He may come to my aid, so that I may be pleasing in His eyes, so that I may delight in His graciousness.' "

— **St. Augustine**

"I speak not, indeed, of such a fast as most persons keep, but of real fasting; not merely an abstinence from meats, but from sins too. . . ."

— **St. John Chrysostom**

139

How to Spend Your Fridays Like a Catholic

Friday — like Sunday — is never an "ordinary" day. Friday is the day when Jesus suffered and died on the cross to atone for our sins. Friday is the day when Jesus won our salvation and made possible our adoption as children of God. Thus, the Church has encouraged us to focus, each Friday, on both gratitude and repentance.

Since Friday is the "anniversary day" of our new life, we should offer extra prayer. We should meditate on the mystery of our redemption, and especially on the sufferings of Christ. When our sinfulness is faced with the love and mercy of God as displayed in the crucifixion, the only appropriate response is repentance — turning away from sin and turning back to God. It is an action of the will, but it should be accompanied by outward expressions. Exercises of piety, almsgiving, and fasting can be signs of true repentance.

Until recently, it was the law of the Church to abstain from meat on Fridays throughout the year. Indeed, from the earliest days, the Church has kept Friday as a day of penance. We find this prescribed in one of the most ancient Christian documents, the *Didache*, composed perhaps within fifty years of Our Lord's Ascension to heaven.

In 1966 the Catholic Bishops of the United States removed the requirement for abstinence from meat on all Fridays of the year. They stated that "the renunciation of the eating of meat is not always and for everyone the most effective means of practicing penance. . . ." In so doing the bishops gave each of us the responsibility that "we discipline ourselves" with forms of fasting and penance that are most meaningful in our own lives.

The Code of Canon Law affirms that Fridays are still days of penance for the whole Church. What we do, however, is up to us. Even today, many families continue to forgo eating meat on Friday. This is a long-revered custom that we would be wise to make our own. We may also choose to make small pilgrimages every Friday, to pray, for example, at a church across town. Or we may take on some special weekly acts of charity.

In 1966 the U.S. bishops wrote: "It would bring greater glory to God and good to souls if Fridays found our people doing volunteer work in hospitals, visiting the sick, serving the needs of the aged and lonely, instructing the young in the faith, participating as Christians in community affairs, and meeting our obligations to our families, our friends, our neighbors, and our community, including our parishes, with a special zeal born of the desire to add the merit of penance to the other virtues exercised in good works born of living faith."

Hold That Thought

Every week, we have an opportunity to establish meaningful penitential practices in individual or family life. Perhaps we could abstain from television on Fridays. Or we can visit the local elder-care home. Personal sacrifices such as fasting and abstinence can be offered along with prayer for others. Recently, the U.S. bishops have suggested that Catholics abstain from meat on Fridays and offer their sacrifice for an end to abortion.

"And He said to all, 'If any man would come after me, let him deny himself and take up his cross daily and follow Me."

— Luke 9:23

141

No Ordinary Day

"Christ died for our salvation on Friday. Gratefully remembering this, Catholic peoples from time immemorial have set apart Friday for special penitential observance by which they gladly suffer with Christ that they may one day be glorified with Him. This is the heart of the tradition of abstinence from meat on Friday where that tradition has been observed in the holy Catholic Church.

"For these and related reasons, the Catholic bishops . . . urge our Catholic people henceforth to be guided by the following norms:

"1. Friday itself remains a special day of penitential observance throughout the year, a time when those who seek perfection will be mindful of their personal sins and the sins of mankind which they are called upon to help expiate in union with Christ Crucified;

"2. Friday should be in each week something of what Lent is in the entire year. For this reason we urge all to prepare for that weekly Easter that comes with each Sunday by freely making of every Friday a day of self-denial and mortification in prayerful remembrance of the Passion of Jesus Christ;

"3. Among the works of voluntary self-denial and personal penance . . . we give first place to abstinence from flesh meat."

**— National Conference of Catholic Bishops,
Norms of Penance and Abstinence,
November 18, 1966**

How to Live Lent

Moses led the Israelites through the desert for forty years. They were traveling to the Promised Land, which flowed with "milk and honey." But strong warrior peoples already held that land. During those forty years in the desert, God formed a people that was both prepared to receive the blessing and ready to do battle against the forces that opposed the establishment of His kingdom. It was a time of purification, instruction, and strengthening.

Jesus spent forty days in the desert in fasting and prayer prior to beginning His public ministry. There He experienced hunger, thirst, and temptation. Scripture tells us that, after this forty days in the desert, Jesus started His ministry "in the power of the Spirit" (Lk 4:14), "from that time Jesus began to preach" (Mt 4:17). The desert experience of prayer and fasting launched Jesus in power into His ministry of proclaiming the Good News, healing the sick, and setting captives free.

Each year, Catholics spend forty days in more intense prayer, fasting, and almsgiving. We call this season Lent. Lent begins on Ash Wednesday. When we go to church that day, the priest traces a cross in ashes on our foreheads. The ashes remind us of two things: that we will one day return to dust, and that we are stained by sin. So we begin Lent by earnestly considering our need for repentance — and the urgency of the matter, since our time on earth is relatively short.

We need then, and throughout Lent, to fix our gaze on the goal of eternal life with the Father — the life made available to us through the resurrection of Jesus, which we celebrate on Easter. Our entire life is a process of conversion, but Lent is the season that allows us to focus more intently on the circumstances of our life in Christ.

The Church earnestly recommends prayer, fasting, and

> "Dear Friends, what the Christian should be doing at all times should be done now with greater care and devotion, so that the Lenten fast enjoined by the apostles may be fulfilled, not simply by abstinence from food but above all by the renunciation of sin."
>
> **— Pope St. Leo the Great**

---

almsgiving as practices appropriate for Lent. These forty days, then, give us a framework for developing our personal devotions. Many parishes offer additional times of prayer, such as communal celebration of the Stations of the Cross, Penance services, and benediction. Church law requires all Catholics fourteen and older to abstain from meat and foods prepared from meat on Ash Wednesday, Good Friday, and all the Fridays of Lent. Catholics aged eighteen to sixty are bound by law also to fast on Ash Wednesday and Good Friday. This means they may only eat two small meals and one larger meal, with no eating between meals. Parishes also take special opportunities for almsgiving, so that we can contribute time, money, and goods for those in need.

But the Church law and parish programs should only be the beginning for us. We should build upon them to make our own personal response to Christ in Lent. We should change our "plan of life" during Lent to make it more demanding, more intensive, better suited to a time of special preparation and penance. We may decide to increase the amount of time we spend at certain devotions, or we may choose to add certain devotions to our plan. We may also choose to take on a special Lenten mortification — giving something up, such as television, candy, or desserts. And, since Lent is a penitential season, sacramental confession should be an important, perhaps weekly or twice-monthly, part of our spiritual program.

Lent is the time when those who wish to enter the Catholic Church undergo a period of intense training culminating with their Baptism at the Easter Vigil. We should pray and offer sacrifices for these new Catholics as they prepare themselves to receive the sacraments.

It's easy for us to grow comfortable in our sin. Lent is a wake-up call. As Lent begins, we should do a penetrating evaluation of our lives. Based on what we find, we should set realistic goals for improvement in virtue, and we should find the means to reach those goals. Some people will do well to fast from complaining. Write yourself a reminder and put it on your mirror or someplace where you will be reminded daily. Ask God for His grace every day. Then, every night review in God's presence how well you've done in your struggle. With a plan and a dedicated pursuit, you will reach Easter a little closer to Our Lord, reflecting His light a little more brightly.

Children should also be taught the value of Lent. They too can offer small sacrifices. The mother of St. Thérèse of Lisieux made "sacrifice beads" for little Thérèse. Every time Thérèse made a little sacrifice out of love of Jesus during the day, she would move a bead. At the end of the day she could "see" her love for Christ. Thérèse attested that this little practice helped her to grow in love for Christ. We too can help children grow closer to Christ by teaching them to offer small sacrifices out of love.

"O Israel, hope in the Lord! / For with the Lord there is steadfast love, / and with Him is plenteous redemption. / And He will redeem Israel / from all his iniquities."

— **Psalm 130:7-8**

(An excellent Lenten meditation.)

Forty Days

"Our fast does not consist chiefly of mere abstinence from food, nor are dainties withdrawn from our bodily appetites with profit unless the mind is recalled from wrongdoing and the tongue restrained from slandering. This is a time of gentleness and long-suffering, of peace and tranquility; when all the pollutions of vice are to be eradicated and continuance of virtue is to be attained by us. Now let godly minds boldly accustom themselves to forgive faults, to pass over insults, and to forget wrongs."

— Pope St. Leo the Great

"Is not this the fast that I choose: to loose the bonds of wickedness, to undo the thongs of the yoke, to let the oppressed go free, and to break every yoke? Is it not to share your bread with the hungry, and bring the homeless poor into your house; when you see the naked, to cover him, and not to hide yourself from your own flesh? Then shall your light break forth like the dawn, and your healing shall spring up speedily; your righteousness shall go before you, the glory of the LORD shall be your rear guard. Then you shall call, and the LORD will answer; you shall cry, and He will say, Here I am."

— Isaiah 58:6-9

How to Make an Act of Contrition

There are many ways to say you're sorry. Any way you express your sorrow to God is called an Act of Contrition. There are several set prayers called by this name. These are the expressions of sorrow that have been most revered by Catholics through history.

The Council of Trent defined contrition as "sorrow of heart and detestation for sin committed, with the resolution not to sin again." Contrition includes, at once, a sorrow for sin, a hatred of sin, and a firm resolve to sin no more. Contrition can be perfect — that is, arising from a love of God. Contrition can also be "imperfect," which means it arises either from a revulsion for the sin or from a fear of punishment. Both forms of contrition are acceptable preludes to sacramental confession.

When we pray an Act of Contrition, there are several principles that we should consider. First, contrition must be interior. In other words, to say the words mechanically with no inner conviction is ineffective. The words of the prayer must reflect the movement of the heart and the will to sorrow and conversion. We need not feel strong emotion, though contrition may include an emotional component.

Also, we need to acknowledge that contrition is supernatural. It is prompted by the grace of God. If someone is sorry for getting drunk simply because the vodka gave him a headache, he is not experiencing true contrition, because his sorrow has a totally natural basis.

Our contrition also needs to be universal. Our sorrow must not be selective. We need to repent of all mortal sins that we are aware of. We can't be sorry for only *some*, because all mortal sins sever our relationship with God. Restoration depends on our true contrition.

The final element of contrition is a "purpose of amendment." As one prayer of contrition states: we firmly resolve, with the help of God's grace, to sin no more and to avoid the near occasions of sin. This resolve includes not only the sin itself but also those situations that generally lead us to commit the sin.

For example, imagine that almost every time you go to a bar with a certain group of people, you end up getting drunk. Then you have to conclude that going to a bar with those individuals is a "near occasion of sin." Thus, it's not enough to want to avoid the sin. We must also plan to avoid the occasions of sin. Certain people, places, and things can be occasions of sin for us. Bad company should be avoided. Certain movies, books, television programs, video games, and internet sites can be occasions of sin. True contrition would resolve to avoid such sources of temptation.

Hold That Thought

It is a good practice to examine your conscience every night and to end with an Act of Contrition. During the day when you are conscious of committing a venial sin, make a quick, sincere Act of Contrition that acknowledges the sin, ask for forgiveness and for strength to avoid the sin the next time.

"[Contrition is] sorrow in the soul and detestation for the sin committed, together with the resolution not to sin again."

— **Council of Trent**

A Broken and Contrite Heart . . .

"So all divines and saints, dealing with contrition and sorrow for sin, advise penitents who are disconsolate because, taking into account the gravity of mortal sins, they cannot burst into tears nor feel in themselves that sensible grief that they would have wished, so that their very hearts should have broken with grief. They tell them, true contrition and sorrow for sin is not in the sensitive appetite, but in the will. Be grieved for having sinned because it is an offense against God, worthy of being loved above all things, for that is true contrition. As for that feeling, when the Lord gives it, receive it gratefully; but when He does not, be not distressed. . . ."

— **Alphonsus Rodriguez**

Prayer

Act of Contrition

O my God, I am heartily sorry for having offended Thee, and I detest all my sins, because I dread the loss of Heaven and the pains of Hell, but most of all because they offend Thee, my God, Who art all-good and deserving of all my love. I firmly resolve, with the help of Thy grace to confess my sins, to do penance, and to amend my life. Amen.

Alternate Act of Contrition

O my God, I am heartily sorry for having offended You. I detest all my sins because of Your just punishments. But most of all because they offend You, my God, Who are all good and deserving of all my love. I firmly resolve with the help of Your grace to sin no more and to avoid the near occasions of sin. Amen.

Eucharistic Devotions

How to Pray the Mass

Prayer doesn't get any better than the Mass.

Since the earliest days of the Church, Christians have considered the Eucharistic liturgy to be both the source and the summit of their life and prayer. How can that be? Because Jesus intended it to be that way. At the Last Supper, Jesus took bread and broke it, saying, "This is My body." He took a cup of wine then, and blessed it calling it the "blood of the covenant" (see Mt 26:26-28). He then commanded His apostles: "Do this in remembrance of me" (1 Cor 11:24-25). Elsewhere, He spoke explicitly of His unique presence in the Eucharist, and its necessity for Christian life: "I am the living bread which came down from heaven; if any one eats of this bread, he will live forever" (Jn 6:51).

In the Eucharist, which we celebrate in the Mass, Christ is made really present under the appearances of bread and wine. After the priest pronounces Jesus' words of consecration — "This is My body . . . This is the cup of My blood" — there is, on the altar, no longer a crumb we can call bread or a drop we can call wine. These elements

have become the Body and Blood of Christ. His presence, from then on, is real and substantial — not symbolic or merely spiritual. Jesus is present with His Body, Blood, soul, and divinity. Some of Jesus' early followers called this doctrine a "hard saying" (see Jn 6:60) and rejected it, but Jesus never backed down. In fact, he spoke of the real presence in ever more graphic terms, as did His apostles and their first followers, whose writings have survived to our own day. We can read of Jesus' real presence in the Eucharist, for example, in the letters of St. Ignatius of Antioch and in a document called the *Didache*, all of which were likely completed before the year 107 A.D.

To grow in faith, we should regularly take the following passages from Scripture to our mental prayer or meditation:

Matthew 26:26-28;
Mark 14:22-24;
Luke 22:19-20;
Luke 24:30-35;
John 6:25-65;
Acts 2:42,46; and
1 Corinthians 11.

It should be clear, then, that the Mass is more than a "service."

• It is the re-presentation of Jesus' sacrifice on the cross, where He poured out His Blood and offered His Body.

• It is our earthly participation in the heavenly liturgy, the marriage supper of the Lamb, which we see in the Book of Revelation (see chapters 4 and 19:6-9).

• It is our thanksgiving to God for all He has given us. (Eucharist literally means "thanksgiving" in Greek).

• It is Jesus Himself, really present as He promised. Thus it is an anticipation of His second coming at the end of time.

The Mass is the most powerful reality we will ever know. Yet we don't always get as much out of it as we would like.

If we're honest, we must admit that we don't always put as much into the Mass as we should. But perhaps we don't know how to put more into our Mass. Consider the following brief counsels, taken from the saints and spiritual masters, and try them out as you have the opportunity.

Now, On Your Way

TRY TO GET TO MASS EARLY. It takes time for us to leave behind all the busyness of the world and turn our attention to Christ in prayer. On finding our place in the church, we should kneel for a moment and make a conscious effort to focus on Jesus. If we're always arriving breathless as Mass begins, we'll likely spend much of the first part of Mass trying to "catch up" with the mystery.

TRY TO ATTEND MASS MORE THAN YOU HAVE TO. All Catholics are required to go to Mass on Sundays and holy days of obligation. But most parishes offer Mass on weekdays as well, and at times convenient to normal work schedules. Weekday Masses are usually quieter, more sparsely attended, and more conducive to attentive prayer. Regular or occasional attendance at weekday Masses can greatly enhance your experience of Sunday Mass.

DRESS UP TO THE OCCASION. There's a natural human tendency to dress up for important events (a job interview or a big date) and dress down for unimportant activities (housework and sports). What we wear can greatly influence how we think and feel. So, when we go to Mass, we should take care with our appearance. We need not wear a tuxedo or evening gown, but we should at least be clean, groomed, and respectably clad. This little effort could make a big difference in the quality of our prayer.

USE A MISSAL. Most churches keep some sort of missal in the pews, so that people can follow the flow of the Mass. Some people find it helpful to read along in the missal as they listen to the prayers and selections from Scripture. It's just another way to focus the mind and the eyes on the matter at hand.

Participate

MAKE THE RESPONSES. It's not enough just to give our minds to the Mass. We have to give our whole selves. God made us body and soul so that we could use both to worship Him. Thus the liturgy engages our senses of touch, taste, hearing, sight, and even smell (if the priest uses incense). The Mass takes up our voices in prayer and our bodies in gestures, such as standing, kneeling, and making the Sign of the Cross.

SING THE SONGS, even if you can't carry a tune. We see in the Book of Revelation that the angels and saints sing around the throne of God in heaven. We on earth would do well to imitate their example. St. Augustine said that to sing is to pray twice. That goes just as well for those who are tone-deaf as for Luciano Pavarotti. Singing can work powerfully to draw you into the drama of the Mass.

FIND TOUCHSTONES. The Mass is made up of distinctive parts. It can help for you to find two or three places where you always "check back in" if your attention has wandered. Consider the following possibilities:

- The "Lord, have mercy." Here's a great opportunity to tell God you're sorry — for gossiping, for lying, for your pride, gluttony, lust, or whatever. Attending Mass and receiving Communion will wipe away all your venial sins.

• The readings. Try to home in on one thing God is trying to tell you in the day's readings. It might be just one word He wants you to focus on.

• The offertory. Here is where we can — silently, in our hearts — place all our ordinary work, conversation, leisure, and family life on the altar with the gifts of bread and wine. God will transform our lives, then, as He transforms the Eucharistic elements.

• The Eucharistic Prayer. After the priest pronounces the words of institution, "This is My Body," he raises up the Host, which has now become the Body of Jesus Christ. After the priest says, "This is My Blood," he will lift up the chalice. At some parishes, an altar server will ring bells to mark these important moments. Some people have the custom, then, of silently acknowledging Jesus' presence by praying, "my Lord and my God."

• Communion. As you're walking to your pew, consider that Jesus Himself is within you now, the same Jesus Who walked the lake shores in Galilee and Who died on a cross for you. Tell Him your most urgent concerns, even if you're angry or disappointed. He is near — He couldn't be nearer — and He is listening in love.

"The same Christ who offered Himself on the Cross, offers Himself up now through the ministry of the priests."

— Council of Trent

BE REVERENT. Reverence does not come naturally to those who live in a democracy where all citizens are considered equals. At the Mass we are all equal before God — but God is infinitely greater than we are. Though He comes to us in intimate love, we should keep in mind that it is an almighty, all-powerful, all-good, and infinite God Who gives Himself to us. That will naturally lead us to. . . .

BE GRATEFUL. Always take time to say "thank you" in the course of the Mass, especially after Communion. One traditional way to express gratitude is to remain at church in silent prayer for a few minutes after Mass has ended.

GIVE YOURSELF WELL. There is no more intimate embrace than the one you experience in the moment of Holy Communion. Whether you receive the Host on your tongue or in your hand, take Jesus with loving care. If you receive on the tongue, put your tongue out far enough so that the priest can easily place the host there, without danger of its falling to the floor. A fifth-century bishop, St. Cyril of Jerusalem, told his congregations the best way to receive Communion was in the hand: "Do not approach with your wrists extended or your fingers spread; but make your left hand a throne for the right, like a throne that is made for a king. And, hollowing your palm, receive the Body of Christ, saying over it, 'Amen.' Then . . . consume [the Host] — carefully, lest you lose any portion. For whatever you lose is your loss, as if it were one of your own limbs. Tell me, if someone gave you grains of gold, wouldn't you hold them with all care, on your guard against losing any? Will you not keep watch more carefully, then, that not a crumb fall from you of what is more precious than gold and precious stones?"

Consider This

To share Himself in the Eucharist was Jesus' most urgent desire on the day He rose from the dead. St. Luke tells of two disciples who were walking that day on the road to Emmaus. They had heard rumors of Jesus' resurrection, but they couldn't believe. Rising from the dead is, after all, an outlandish claim. So, as they walked, they mourned and tried to imagine what life would be like now that their Master was dead.

Along the way, they were joined by a stranger, a man Who listened to their grieving, but, finally, refused to let them wallow in it. Calling them "foolish," He went on to interpret for them the passages that referred to Jesus in all the Old Testament. When the three travelers arrived at the village, the disciples begged the man to stay with them. He did.

And then came the clincher: "At table, He took bread, said the blessing, broke it, and gave it to them. With that, their eyes were opened and they recognized Him" (Lk 24:30-31 NAB). It was Jesus! "Then they said to each other, 'Were not our hearts burning [within us] while He spoke to us on the way and opened the Scriptures to us" (Lk 24:32). They went then to Jerusalem, where they told what had happened and how Jesus "was made known to them in the breaking of the bread'" (Lk 24:35).

This is the course of every Mass for the believing Catholic. We arrive, perhaps distracted and downcast by our sins. But in the Mass, Jesus confronts us with our foolishness and gives us an opportunity to repent. He opens up the Scriptures for us. Finally, we know Him in the breaking of the bread.

This is how the first Christians knew Him. This is how every generation of Christians has known Him. This is how all faithful Christians will know Him in heaven. In the Eucharist, Jesus gives us Himself in all His glory. We receive heaven in its entirety. All of the promises of Christ are fulfilled in every Mass — the re-presentation of Calvary, the marriage supper of the Lamb. If we open our hearts to the Scripture, He will make our hearts burn within us. If we open our eyes to His presence, we will know Him, and we will need nothing else.

Know Him in the Mass

"And Jesus said 'Father, if it be possible, let this cup pass from Me.' The cup of our salvation was a bitter cup for Him to drink. And when the priest (at the offertory of the Mass) asks God to accept the cup of salvation, shall we think about the cup which Our Lord thought about at Gethsemani, and offer up our lives with it, as He offered up His life in Gethsemani: 'Nevertheless not my will, but Thine, be done!' "

— **Ronald Knox**

"My God and my Savior, of all the wonderful gifts which You have bestowed upon men in this earthly life, none can begin to compare with the wonderful gift of the Holy Eucharist. Under the appearances of bread and wine, You come to me in person, with Your body, blood, soul, and divinity. Your love for me is so deep that You could offer me nothing less than Yourself. This You did in a manner which reminds me of Your death upon the cross for my sake. In the appearance of bread and wine I see You ready to be consumed in order to give me eternal life. This holy sacrament is truly the most perfect image of Your boundless love for me. Lord, let me make full use of this divine gift so that I may learn to give myself to You in my daily life. Amen."

— **Anthony J. Paone, S.J.**

Devoutly I adore You, hidden Deity,
You Who truly lie hid under these species;
To You my heart submits completely,
Because in contemplating You it fails totally.

Sight, touch, and taste in You are each deceived;
By hearing alone it suffices firmly to believe;
I believe whatever said the Son of God:
Nothing is truer than the word of Truth.

On the cross Divinity alone lie hid,
Yet here Humanity as well is hidden:
Both, however, believing and confessing
I seek what the repentant thief sought.

Your wounds, as Thomas, I do not gaze upon,
My God, however I confess You to be.
In You, make me more and more to believe,
In You to have hope, You to love deeply.

O memorial of the death of Our Lord!
Living Bread granting life to man!
Grant my soul to live on You,
And grant it always You sweetly discern.

    — *Adoro te devote*, St. Thomas Aquinas

How to Make a Holy Hour

In the Garden of Gethsemane Jesus experienced bitter pain and anguish as He prepared for His Passion and death. Many spiritual writers suggest that a part of that pain and anguish arose because Jesus was able to see all of those who would reject His love and salvation. He also could see the many sins and offenses that would be committed by His followers despite the grace He was to make available to them. Jesus had taken His closest friends with Him to this place of prayer. He had asked them to keep watch and pray that "you may not enter into temptation" (Lk 22:40). However the disciples could not remain awake, so they slept while Jesus was "greatly distressed and troubled" (Mk 14:33). When Jesus saw them sleeping He said: "Are you asleep? Could you not watch for one hour?" (Mk 14:37).

Certainly we are busy. There are many demands on our time. However, Our Lord remains faithfully present in the Eucharist that is reserved in the tabernacles of the churches. He, a willing "prisoner of love," awaits us. He sees the sins of the world and offers forgiveness, grace, and life. He waits. Can we not wait with Him for one hour?

Churches throughout the world have established programs of perpetual adoration before the Blessed Sacrament. People volunteer for one hour per week to be with Jesus Who is truly present in the tabernacle. Many of these programs are in need of additional people to take one hour a week to spend with Our Lord.

Why spend a holy hour before Jesus in the Blessed Sacrament? There is only one answer and it is simple. Jesus Christ, the God-Man, is present. As St. Thomas Aquinas said: "He cares for us and is there."

If this is a once-a-week devotion for you (it can be more often!), it is valuable to establish a specific day and time. Treat it as an appointment you have made with your friend, Jesus. You would not want to "stand up" your friend.

How to spend that hour in prayer? There is no set formula. You can use a prayer book or the Bible to help you. You can meditate or just sit and enjoy the peace that comes from resting in the presence of God. One man described to St. John Vianney his time of prayer before the tabernacle as: "I look at Him Whom I love and He looks at me."

Whatever your approach and it probably will help to try different ones in the beginning, it's important not to become discouraged. We are among the most over-stimulated generations in the world's history. Silence, contemplation, inviting Christ to enter our hearts and minds can seem alien to us, foolish, and difficult. Almost all of us, in the beginning, will want to fidget. Almost all will experience wandering thoughts, even

"How great is the value of conversation with Christ in the Blessed Sacrament, for there is nothing more consoling on earth, nothing more efficacious for advancing along the road to holiness!"

— Pope Paul VI

---

temptations! Don't worry, they don't matter. All that matters is that you are there, and you are there with good intent.

We have forgotten as Christians how much God loves a pure heart, or even an impure heart that we have only begun to ask Him to purify. God is not terribly impressed by our success (since He is the author of all success) but He loves it when we try. In the end if we make a distracted, worried, or sleepy holy hour we do much better than if we not make any at all.

One approach is to divide the hour into fifteen-minute segments. This is handy because it's possible to start not with an hour but with the first fifteen minutes. Take the first fifteen minutes to meditate upon Him Who is present in the Holy Eucharist. Consider the marvel of this reality: Christ the God-Man is truly present in His divinity as well as in His sacred humanity. He is present body and soul. Try to realize how this unique presence of Jesus in the tabernacle is different from the presence of God in the world, or from His presence in us by grace, or from His presence in the Church or in Scripture. Jesus in the Blessed Sacrament is unique — different from His presence anywhere else.

Consider Who Jesus is as God: Creator, Redeemer, Savior, our Brother, Our Lord and King of the universe. Join familiar prayers of worship with your thoughts. Reflect on the words of some hymns of praise and adoration such as: "Down in Adoration Falling," "Holy God, We Praise Thy Name," "Now Thank We All Our God," etc. Read the words slowly and thoughtfully. Pause and allow your heart to embrace Him Who resides in the tabernacle.

For the second fifteen minutes turn to prayers of thanksgiving. Give thanks to God for His presence in the Eucharist. Thank Our Lord for the Mass, the Sacraments, the Church, and the priesthood. Use the Magnificat or the Canticle of Zachary as helps in your thanksgiving. Recall His blessings to you: family, vocation, the gift of life, opportunity to be in His presence, friends, benefactors, etc. Thank Him for the help He provides in struggles and temptations.

Dedicate the third segment of the holy hour to prayers of petition. Pray first that God's will be done in your life and in the lives of those closest to you. Remember the needs of family and friends, and bring forth the needs of the Church both local and universal. Pray for your pastor, the bishop, and the pope. You may also pray for conversions and for the return to the faith of those who have wandered. Include prayer for the sick, the lonely, the discouraged, young people, the unborn, government officials, co-workers. Pray that you may know God's will and may be a channel of His grace to others. Pray for peace. Know that He hears your prayers. You can believe Jesus when He tells us: "Come to Me all you who labor and are burdened and I will refresh you!"

"Eucharistic Adoration offers to our people the opportunity to join those in religious life to pray for the salvation of the world, souls everywhere and peace on earth. We cannot underestimate the power of prayer and the difference it will make in our world."

— **Mother Teresa of Calcutta**

Let the final quarter of your time be set aside for "atonement." Sin is a grave offense to the justice of God. Jesus gave His life on the cross to atone for the sins and offenses of man. He invites us to join in His atonement. Consider your own sins, and the insults, blasphemies, and defiance of men and women of our world in the face of the love of God. How often is love of neighbor ignored or even contradicted by abortion, hate, and immorality! Express your thoughts of sorrow to God. Say an Act of Contrition. The Litany of the Sacred Heart, the Litany of the Holy Name, and the Litany of the Blessed Mother are all helpful prayers. The Litany to the Saints and the Prayer to St. Michael can also be used.

A holy hour spent before Our Lord in the tabernacle is time well spent. However, a holy hour can be observed at home. Sometimes family situations make it impossible to observe the hour at Church. It may be too difficult for smaller children. At home the prayer can be structured to include the children in singing of hymns and recitation of the family Rosary. Unite your prayer to Jesus Who resides in the Church tabernacle closest to your home — perhaps even facing in the direction of the Church as you pray.

The aged, sick, and handicapped are often unable to spend a holy hour at church. However, their prayer from home, when united with the offering of their infirmities, can be a powerful instrument for the work of God's grace. Many souls have been saved through the faithful prayer of those who are homebound.

Some may ask: What is the effect of a regular holy hour and the practice of other Eucharistic devotions? Isn't it somewhat a waste of time to spend an hour in Church when it could be used for more active "work"? Recall the story of the apostles in the Scripture when they spent the entire night fishing. With their best efforts they caught nothing (Lk 5:1-7). When Jesus arrived He ordered them to cast in their nets one more time. Their catch was so great that it "filled both boats, so that they began to sink." The presence of Jesus brought a superabundance of life and blessing for the apostles.

It is the same with us. Our efforts in the work of God are important but unless Jesus is present and directing our action, there will be no results. As we spend time in the presence of Jesus, miracles can happen. As we spend time before the tabernacle, we will grow in love of the Eucharist, and love for souls will be given us. Our hearts will be caught up in the work, life, and love of God.

Hold That Thought

Pope John Paul II has been a strong proponent of Eucharistic devotion. The primary devotion is the Mass. Attendance at this divine banquet should be the center of our Eucharistic devotion. However, love of Our Lord in the Blessed Sacrament impels us to worship Him present in the tabernacle.

The Solemnity of the Body and Blood of Christ (celebrated in the United States on the Sunday after Trinity Sunday) focuses our attention on the Body of Christ in the Eucharist. Special Eucharistic devotion is often celebrated with this feast including benediction and Eucharistic processions. In some countries, these processions are solemn parades that go through the center of the town or village.

Various parishes also hold yearly Eucharistic days when special devotion is center upon Jesus in the Eucharist. Benediction and public Eucharistic devotions give us the opportunity for a corporate expression of our love for Christ in the Eucharist.

As evil grows in our society, the power of the Eucharist becomes more evident as the source of good, life and hope.

"The Eucharist is what is most real in the world."

— **François Mauriac**

The Body and Blood

"Your faith will help you to realize that it is Jesus Himself Who is present in the Blessed Sacrament, waiting for you and calling you to spend one special specific hour with Him each week."

— Pope John Paul II

"People ask me: 'What will convert America and save the world?' My answer is prayer. What we need is for every parish to come before Jesus in the Blessed Sacrament in Holy Hours of prayer."

— Mother Teresa of Calcutta

Jesus Waits for Us Here
With Divine Longing

Adore and visit Jesus, abandoned and forsaken
by men in His Sacrament of Love.
Man has time for everything
except for visits to His Lord and God,
Who is waiting and longing for us
in the Blessed Sacrament.
The streets and places of entertainment
are filled with people;
the House of God is deserted.
Men flee from it; they are afraid of it.
Ah! Poor Jesus!
Did You expect so much indifference
from those You have redeemed,
from Your friends, from Your children, from me?

Sympathize with Jesus Who is betrayed,
insulted, mocked, and crucified far more ignominiously
in His Sacrament of Love than He was
in the Garden of Olives, in Jerusalem, and on Calvary.
Those whom He has the most honored, loved,
and enriched with His gifts and graces
are the very ones who offend Him the most
by their indifference.

Offer up for this intention all that you have suffered
during the day or week
that Jesus may be loved and adored by all.
Because we ourselves are unable to atone for
so much wrong,
we unite ourselves
to the infinite merits of our Savior Jesus.
Receive His Divine Blood
as it mystically flows from His Holy Wounds,
and offer it to the Father
in perfect atonement for the sins of the world.

Take His sufferings
and His prayer on the Cross
and beg the Heavenly Father
for pardon and mercy for all.

Unite your reparation
to that of the most Blessed Virgin
at the foot of the Cross or the altar,
and from the love of Jesus for His Divine Mother
you will obtain everything.

— **St. Peter Julian Eymard**

The King of Love My Shepherd Tis

The King of Love my Shepherd is,
Whose goodness fails me never;
I nothing lack if I am His,
And He is mine forever.

Where streams of living water flow
With gentle care He leads me,
And where the verdant pastures grow
With heav'nly food He feeds me.

Perverse and foolish I have strayed
But yet in love He sought me,
And on His shoulder gently laid,
And home, rejoicing, brought me.

In death's dark vale I fear no ill
With You, dear Lord, beside me,
Your rod and staff my comfort still,
Your Cross before to guide me.

You spread a table in my sight,
Your saving grace bestowing;
And O what joy and true delight
From Your pure chalice flowing!

And so through all the length of days
Your goodness fails me never;
Good Shepherd, may I sing Your praise
Within Your house forever.

— St. Columba

How to Make
a Eucharistic "Visit"

Friendship is a rare commodity in today's fast-paced society. With our busy work schedules, we have less time to visit with others just to enjoy their company. Yet we continue to hunger for friendship.

At its root, that hunger is our desire for the presence and friendship of Jesus Christ. To fulfill that need is a matter of His grace and our initiative. We need to visit Jesus, as we would visit any friend, and we need to visit Him often, as we would drop in on our best friends.

Jesus remains really present in the tabernacle of every Catholic Church. The tabernacle is the place within the church where the Eucharist is reserved for adoration and for distribution to people who are homebound or hospitalized. Usually, a candle — called the sanctuary lamp — is kept near the tabernacle, to signify Jesus' abiding presence there.

Many Catholics practice the tradition of "making visits" to Jesus in the tabernacle. All this means is that they stop in the church at a time apart from Mass, for the express purpose of prayer. A visit need not be long — maybe just a few minutes. It can be like a brief visit to an old friend.

Every Eucharistic visit should begin with a genuflection, which is the traditional sign of reverence before the tabernacle. Whenever we pass before the real presence of Christ, we should drop to kneel on our right knee; remain kneeling that way for a brief moment; then rise again.

After that, our Eucharistic visit could take any form. We might use formal prayers, such as the Our Father, Hail Mary, and Glory Be. We might offer prayers of aspiration. Or we might just silently pray to Jesus in our own words.

If there is a church near where you work, perhaps you

could make a visit on your lunch hour. Or on your way home from work or school, you can make the trip include a quick stop before the tabernacle — time enough to greet the Savior and know His presence and love. It's a daily routine that helps keep a relationship strong and a life oriented in the ways of God.

Hold That Thought

One father of a large family, happily married for twenty-five years, credited the blessing of his vocation to Eucharistic visits. He states: "When I was in grade school I would stop in church for a visit after class and before I returned home. I would kneel at the altar rail and ask God to direct me in the vocation He desired for my life. He honored that prayer and blessed me in abundance."

Treasure the Moment

"The visit to the Blessed Sacrament is a great treasure of the Catholic faith. It nourishes social love and gives us opportunities for adoration and thanksgiving, for reparation and supplication."

— Pope John Paul II

"Jesus has made Himself the Bread of Life to give us life. Night and day, He is there. If you really want to grow in love, come back to the Eucharist, come back to that Adoration."

— Mother Teresa of Calcutta

"God dwells in our midst, in the Blessed Sacrament of the altar."

— St. Maximilian Kolbe

Prayers

Eucharistic Prayer of Mother Teresa of Calcutta

"O God, we believe You are here. We adore You and love You with our whole heart and soul because You are most worthy of all our love. We desire to love You as the Blessed do in Heaven. . . . Flood our souls with Your spirit and life. Penetrate and possess our whole being utterly, that our lives may only be a radiance of Yours. Shine through us, and be so in us, that every soul we come in contact with may feel Your presence in our soul. Let them look up and see no longer us, but only Jesus!"

Prayer of the Angel at Fátima

O Most Holy Trinity, Father,
Son, and Holy Spirit,
I adore Thee profoundly.
I offer Thee the most precious
Body, Blood, Soul, and Divinity
of Jesus Christ,
present in all the tabernacles
of the world, in reparation
for the outrages, sacrileges,
and indifference by which
He is offended.
By the infinite merits
of the Sacred Heart of Jesus and
the Immaculate Heart of Mary,
I beg Thee the conversion of poor sinners.

Prayer of the Holy Father

" 'Lord stay with us.' These words were spoken for the first time by the disciples of Emmaus. Subsequently in the course of the centuries they have been spoken, an infinite number of times, by the lips of so many of Your disciples and confessors, O Christ.

"As Bishop of Rome and first servant of this temple, which stands on the place of St. Peter's martyrdom, I speak the same words today.

"I speak then to invite You, Christ, in Your Eucharistic Presence to accept the daily adoration continuing through the entire day, in this temple, in this basilica, in this chapel.

"Stay with us today and stay, from now on, every day, according to the desire of my heart, which accepts the appeal of so many hearts from various parts, sometimes far away, and above all meets the desire of so many inhabitants of the Apostolic See.

"Stay! That we may meet You in the prayer of adoration and thanksgiving, in the prayer of expiation and petition, to which all those who visit this basilica are invited.

"Stay! You Who are at one and the same time veiled in the Eucharistic Mystery of Faith and are also revealed under the species of bread and wine, which You have assumed in this Sacrament.

"Stay! That Your presence in this temple may incessantly be reconfirmed, and that all those who enter here may become aware that it is Your house, 'the dwelling of God with men' (Rev 21:3) and, visiting this basilica, may find in it the very source of life and holiness that gushes forth from Your Eucharistic Heart. . . .

'One day, O Lord, You asked Peter: 'Do you love Me?' You asked him three times — and three times the apostle answered: "Lord, You know everything, You know that I love You" (Jn 21:15-17).'

172

"May the answer of Peter, on whose tomb this basilica was erected, be expressed by this daily and daylong adoration which we have begun today.

"May the unworthy successor of Peter in the Roman See — and all those who take part in the adoration of Your Eucharistic Presence — attest with every visit of theirs and make ring out again the truth contained in the apostle's words:

" 'Lord You know everything; You know that I love You.' Amen."

— Pope John Paul II, inaugurating Perpetual Eucharistic Adoration at St. Peter's at the beginning of Advent, 1981

Abide With Us

"Do you realize that Jesus is there in the tabernacle expressly for you   for you alone? He burns with the desire to come into your heart . . . don't listen to the demon, laugh at him, and go without fear to receive the Jesus of peace and love. . . ."

— St. Thérèse of Lisieux

"He remains among us until the end of the world. He dwells on so many altars, though so often offended and profaned."

— St. Maximilian Kolbe

How to Keep the Lord's Day Holy

The Bible is very specific. It is one of the Ten Commandments to keep holy the sabbath. Throughout the Old Testament God continued to call His people to faithful observance of "the Lord's Day." When they drifted from this commandment, they also drifted from other commitments to God. For the Jewish people the Sabbath coincided with the day of creation when God rested.

With the death and resurrection of Christ, the Church transferred the observance of a day dedicated to God to Sunday, the day of the resurrection triumph of Jesus. Therefore, for the Christian, Sunday is an opportunity to ponder and grow in the life of Easter, the source of the world's salvation.

The focus of our Sunday worship is the Mass. We gather together as the family of God to be fed on the Bread of Life. It is a sign of our unity in Christ that, just as the first disciples did, we gather to break bread. Pope John Paul II emphasized the unitive aspects of the Sunday Eucharist when he wrote: "It is normal to find different groups, movements, associations, and even smaller religious groups present in the parish. However Sunday is the day for all Catholics to gather as one in the family of God" ("On Keeping the Lord's Day Holy," no. 36).

Together as the People of God at Mass, we receive the Word of God in the Scriptures. We are prepared to go forth to the tasks that will face us in the coming week. Spiritually, we are refreshed and strengthened by the Eternal Word, Christ, Who comes to us in His word and in the Eucharist.

Even though joining together at Mass is the heart of Sunday, "the duty to keep Sunday holy cannot be reduced to this" ("On Keeping. . ." no. 52). It is also to be a day of active remembrance when we gratefully recall the saving work of Christ. We are to shape other parts of our day "in such a way that the peace and joy of the Risen Lord will emerge in the ordinary events of life . . . family life, social relationships, moments of relaxation" ("On Keeping . . ." no. 52).

The Church encourages families to draw together on Sunday "not only to listen to one another but also to share a few formative and reflective moments" ("On Keeping . . ." no. 52). Special times of prayer in addition to the Mass are encouraged. Pope John Paul II suggests a Sunday pilgrimage to some local shrine that would include the entire family.

The physical and mental rest that the Church encourages on Sunday provides an opportunity for Christians to develop a better perspective on our daily concerns and tasks.

Finally, our observance of Sunday should include a concern for the needy in our midst. This tradition is rooted in apostolic times. There are sick, lonely, and isolated people living in our neighborhoods. There are needy people among the elderly and children. Sunday often gives us time to reach out in a personal way to those around us. "Why not make the Lord's Day a more intense time of sharing, encouraging all the inventiveness of which Christian charity is capable? Inviting to a meal people who are alone, visiting the sick, providing food for needy families, spending a few hours in voluntary work and acts of solidarity: these would certainly be ways of bringing into people's lives the love of Christ received at the Eucharistic table" ("On Keeping . . ." no. 72).

Consider This

Sunday affords a wonderful opportunity to learn more about the faith. You can spend an extended time in reading or studying. There are many good Catholic books that are now available at reasonable prices — classical works by the Fathers, lives of the saints, and works by contemporary authors. One good Sunday reading would be the letter by Pope John Paul II mentioned above entitled "On Keeping the Lord's Day Holy" (*Dies Domini* is the Latin title). Although the Holy Father addresses himself in particular to the bishops in this letter, there is much information on which we can contemplate.

Also on Sunday we can spend extra time in prayer and meditation. One suggestion would be to read the Scriptures for that Sunday and spend time in prayer with them. We can also involve all the family by having a discussion of those Scriptures.

In many ways we need to recapture Sunday as a celebration of the Day of the Lord. Western society no longer supports us in this approach. For many it is just another workday. The *Catechism of the Catholic Church* urges us to limit work and business activities.

Sunday can be viewed as "family" day. We gather at Mass with the family of God. At home the domestic church can gather on Sunday. A Sunday family meeting allows time for dealing with family issues. It can also be a wonderful opportunity for parents to exercise their role as the primary educators of their children. Informal classes should be age-specific. They can range from how to behave at Mass and how to answer the telephone to subjects such as the sacraments.

Remember the Lord's Day . . .

"Remember the sabbath day, to keep it holy. Six days you shall labor, and do all your work; but the seventh day is a sabbath to the LORD your God; in it you shall not do any work, you, or your son, or your daughter, your man-servant, or your maidservant, or your cattle, or the so-journer who is within your gates; for in six days the LORD made heaven and earth, the sea, and all that is in them, and rested the seventh day; therefore the LORD blessed the sabbath day and hallowed it."

— **Exodus 20:8-11**

"And [Jesus] said to them, 'The sabbath was made for man, not man for the sabbath; so the Son of man is lord even of the sabbath.' "

— **Mark 2:27-28**

"And on the day of Our Lord's resurrection, which is the Lord's day, meet more diligently, sending praise to God Who made the universe by Jesus, and sent Him to us, and condescended to let Him suffer, and raised Him from the dead. Otherwise what apology will he make to God Who does not assemble on that day to hear the saving word concerning the resurrection. . . ?'"

— **From the *Didache* (circa 80 A.D.)**

... Keep It Holy

"Sanctifying Sundays and holy days requires a common effort. Every Christian should avoid making unnecessary demands on others that would hinder them from observing the Lord's Day. Traditional activities (sports, restaurants, etc.), and social necessities (public services, etc.), require some people to work on Sundays, but everyone should still take care to set aside sufficient time for leisure."

— CCC, no. 2187

". . . Sunday is traditionally consecrated by Christian piety to good works and humble service of the sick, the infirm, and the elderly. Christians will also sanctify Sunday by devoting time and care to their families and relatives, often difficult to do on other days of the week. Sunday is a time for reflection, silence, cultivation of the mind, and meditation which furthers the growth of the Christian interior life."

— CCC, no. 2186

"Thanks, then, to the Lord our God Who accomplished a work in which He might find rest. He made the heavens, but I do not read that He found rest there; He made the stars, the moon, the sun, and neither do I read that He found rest in them. I read instead that He made man and then He rested, finding in man one to whom He could offer the forgiveness of sins."

— St. Ambrose

Sacramentals and Blessings

How to Pray With Sacred Images

If you are like most people, it is safe to assume that somewhere in your purse or wallet, you have some family pictures. Why do you bother to carry them with you? Well, if you are a grandparent you may want to use them to prove that you have the best-looking grandkids! More likely, though, you carry them because you carry your family with you in your heart and mind always. When you look at those pictures it touches a wealth of lived experience — joys and sorrows — that you connect with the people in those pictures. It also recalls the hopes and aspirations that you have for those family members. When you look at that picture, don't you feel a closeness to them as well as a longing to be near them?

There is a real parallel between those pictures in your purse and the statues and paintings that we see at church or display in our homes. Holy images are of many varieties. There is artwork that depicts events from the life of Christ, the portrait of a saint, or a symbol of some aspect

179

of the faith. We can discuss several of the beneficial aspects of the use of these images in Christian prayer: focus, teaching, imitation, and devotion.

We are not angels! Angels are pure spirits. They do not deal with the senses of sight, touch, hearing, smell, and taste. We human beings, however, are not pure spirit. We have a body, a God-given body. Therefore our senses were a part of God's intent for man. As with any gift, sinful man can abuse and misuse it. However, used rightly, those gifts of our senses bring us closer to the Gift Giver. The sacraments and sacramentals of the Church all have a sensory component that helps us identify with the spiritual. The aroma of incense and the rising smoke that may be used at Mass or benediction help us to realize that our prayers and offerings rise to God as a sweet aroma. Also, incense is a material saved for special occasions and, therefore, reminds us of the honor due God. Incense then helps us to focus and pray.

Holy images have a similar purpose. When we look at the crucifix, it reminds us of the sacrifice of Jesus. Our thoughts may have been wandering, but when we see the crucifix, we are able to refocus and return to prayer. As our physical eyes look at the statue, painting, card, or other image it helps the "eyes" of our heart and mind to turn to Him Who is represented in the artwork.

Through history many images were also meant to instruct the faithful. When reading and books were not accessible to the masses, the artwork in the church was a teaching tool. In fact, the Gothic cathedral has been referred to as the "gospel in stone." Every aspect of the architecture and artwork was meant to teach and raise the mind and heart to consideration of the Savior and the truths of the faith. The grandeur of the cathedral itself created an awe that pointed to the grandeur of God and the worship that was due to Him alone.

Images of saints help develop devotion to the saint, but also serve as an encouragement to imitate the virtues of that particular saint. Many men will keep an image of St. Joseph in a conspicuous place so that they will be reminded both to imitate his example as a husband and father and be reminded to ask his intercession for those same petitions. Many priests will keep an image of St. John Vianney in their office. Again, they ask the intercession of the patron of priests that they may imitate his example.

Holy images can also help to increase our devotion and cultivate piety. When a husband looks at the picture of his wife, he renews his love for her. When we see the image of Our Lord or of one of the saints, it provides the opportunity for us to renew our love and commitment.

The use of images has its roots in the Old Testament. The ark of the covenant, the bronze serpent raised up in the camp by Moses, and the temple building are all examples of tangible items that were used in the Old Testament to help the Israelites to focus on God and to worship Him.

"The Christian veneration of images is not contrary to the first commandment which proscribes idols. Indeed, 'the honor rendered to an image passes to its prototype,' and 'whoever venerates an image venerates the person portrayed in it.' "

— CCC, no. 2132

There is no one way to pray with images. A lot depends on the person using the image and which image he or she is using. In many ways, the first step in praying with images is to choose the image you wish to contemplate in prayer. Catholic bookstores and gift shops usually sell religious art, including statues, medals, paintings, and photographs. A few also have outlets on the World Wide Web.

When choosing an image, don't rush your purchase. Study the artwork a bit. Which ones seem to "speak" to you? Is there one or two or three to which you feel particularly drawn and, if there is more than one, is there one among them that seems to attract you more than the others? Look at the eyes. Notice whether Christ is seated or standing, whether a saint holds a book or a flower or a baby. All those things have meaning related to the life of Christ or the saint.

Once you have chosen an image, bring it home and set it in a quiet place. Study the face depicted there. Consciously put yourself in God's presence, asking Him to invite you closer through this image. Then take up whatever method of prayer seems most natural. Some people pray with an image at night, reviewing their day while facing a vivid reminder of Christ or a saint. Some people offer a Rosary or other devotion. Whatever you do, it is liable to be a different experience when you do it under the gaze of a sacred image.

Hold That Thought

There are many ways that holy images can help us to both pray and grow in devotion. One family, realizing that it was often difficult to turn off the television, placed a statue of the Sacred Heart of Jesus on top of the set. They made a conscious decision that they would not watch any program that would offend God and grieve the heart of Jesus. That statue was a silent but powerful reminder of their decision and helped them to keep it.

To pray in front of an image of Our Lord helps you to keep the focus on Him during prayer. A small crucifix on the desk at work or above the machine in the factory or at the kitchen stove will help you to recollect. Images in a Christian home give witness to the faith of those who live there — and also serve as a reminder to each family member of Who is the Lord of the home.

Another pious practice is to establish a "family altar" in the home. A particular corner of a room is set aside for the altar. On a small table is placed some Holy images — usually a crucifix and a statue of the Blessed Mother. The altar has a place of honor in the home. Here the family can gather for prayers, perhaps to say the Rosary or night prayers together. Each time the family gathers in that room, it reminds them that Jesus is also present.

Some people will keep a small image of a saint or a crucifix inside their car, perhaps on the dashboard. This image can remind the driver to begin travel with a prayer for God's protection. Also, in these days of "road rage," that image may remind us that love of neighbor is a commandment of God — even when that neighbor is the driver of the car behind or in front of us!

Praying With Sacred Images

"The images of Christ, of the Virgin Mother of God, and of the other saints, are to be placed and retained especially in the churches, and that due honor and veneration be extended to them, not that any divinity or virtue is believed to be in them . . . but because the honor which is shown them, is referred to the prototypes which they represent, so that by means of the images, which we kiss and before which we bare the head and prostrate ourselves, we adore Christ, and venerate the saints, whose likeness they bear."

— The Council of Trent

"Catholics do not worship the Cross or images or relics. They use these physical objects to remind themselves of Christ and His special friends, the saints in heaven."

**— From *Catholicism and Fundamentalism*
by Karl Keating**

How to Make a Consecration

"Consecration" is not a word that is likely to appear in our everyday conversations. In fact, it has lost much of its meaning in contemporary understanding. The word "consecration" comes from the root word that means *holy*. Fundamentally it means that a person, place, or thing is sanctified —made holy — to the Lord. Something that is common and profane becomes dedicated to the service and worship of God.

In the Old Testament Solomon built a temple to the Lord. Upon completion there was an elaborate service in which the temple was dedicated to the Lord, described in chapter five of 2 Chronicles. As the service progressed "the building of the Lord's temple was filled with a cloud . . . the Lord's glory filled the house" (2 Chr 5:13-14). At this point the consecration of the building had occurred. The people had offered the building to God for His service and His holy presence had become manifest.

The Church has followed the example of the Old Testament and has special services to consecrate persons, places and things to the Lord and specifically for His work. Thus there is a consecration for a Church and a consecration service for the elevation of a new bishop.

There is actually only one Who is holy: God Himself. All other holiness has its origin in Him. Since consecration involves the designation of a place or person as "holy," it is God alone Who can "consecrate." We are all consecrated to God through Baptism. We become "temples of the Holy Spirit." Just as the presence of the Lord inhabited Solomon's temple, so also God takes up residence in the new Christian in the Sacrament of Baptism.

Baptism is referred to as objective consecration. That means God's presence designates us as holy. When you read the epistles of Paul, he regularly refers to the believ-

> "Till now you have taken the name my slave. From now on, you shall be called the well beloved disciple and My Sacred Heart."
>
> **— Our Lord to St. Margaret Mary Alacoque**

---

ers as "the holy ones." This is true because The Holy One, God Himself, has made it so. As St. Paul writes to the believers: "The temple of God, which you are, is holy."

Consecration has been taught by a number of saints and popes. Of note is the practice of dedication of a person or a family to the Sacred Heart of Jesus. Saints such as Bonaventure, Catherine of Siena, Francis de Sales, and John Eudes promoted this devotion. In the seventeenth century St. Margaret Mary Alacoque received visions of Our Lord in which He encouraged dedication and devotion to His love and mercy as expressed in His Sacred Heart. Our Lord also gave twelve "promises" to those who were devoted to His Sacred Heart.

Several popes including Pius IX, Leo XIII, and Pius XI explicitly endorsed the devotion. In fact in 1899 Pope Leo XIII took the action of formally consecrating the entire world to the Sacred Heart. By so doing the Holy Father was proclaiming that God already has full rights over us and that we owe Him everything.

The consecration of a family to the Sacred Heart of Jesus usually occurs within the context of a "home enthronement." This short prayer service is available at many Catholic bookstores. The family sets aside a specific time for the ceremony, perhaps on a Sunday. Family members may wish to dress in their "Sunday best" clothes to emphasize the importance of the occasion. Members gather at a convenient place in the home and place some image of the Sacred Heart of Jesus in their midst. The image could be a statue, a portrait, or merely a card with the image of Jesus. The image helps the family focus attention upon the Lord.

The service will include a Scripture reading such as Deuteronomy 7:6-11, which calls to mind God's election of His people and His call to them to be obedient to His commands. The father or mother of the family often gives a short reflection on the meaning of the ceremony, on the Scripture or on the twelve promises (listed on page 191). A responsorial psalm and various intercessions for the family may follow. All members of the family participate. Next the family processes to a place of honor where the image of the Sacred Heart will be placed. Lighted candles and song add solemnity to the procession.

At the location where the image will be "enthroned" the family joins together in praying the prayer of consecration (printed on page 192). The service may end with the praying of the Our Father, Hail Mary, and Glory Be. A family meal or shared refreshments make an appropriate follow-up activity.

The image remains at the location as a constant reminder to the family of the mercy, love, and protection of Christ. The image also serves to remind all that this is a Christian home that has placed Jesus at the center — on the throne — of the family.

A renewal of the consecration is held annually on the anniversary of the original enthronement or on the Feast of Christ the King or on the Feast of the Sacred Heart (June 11).

An individual can use a similar approach. Again this subjective consecration ties to the objective consecration that occurs through our entry into the life of Christ in Baptism. It gives families and individuals the opportunity

---

"All our perfection consists in being conformed, united and consecrated to Jesus Christ."

— St. Louis Marie de Montfort

to respond in a concrete way to a commitment to God.

The saints offer examples of lives that were committed to God in profound ways. They lived consecrated lives. Their example and intercession can assist us to live similar lives. Therefore the practice of consecration to a particular saint has grown over the years. For example, there is a consecration to St. Joseph. However, the most common such consecration is the Consecration to Mary. More precisely it is called Consecration to Jesus through Mary.

Since God is the source of all holiness, any consecration must have Him as the focus. Mary's life is the prototype of the perfect consecration. When God called her through the angel Gabriel to be the mother of the Savior, her response was "I am the handmaid of the Lord. May it be done to me according to your word!" Mary's "fiat" (i.e. let it be done) in response to God's will for her life shows us the way to consecrate our lives to Him. Also Mary continued that "fiat" throughout her life. Her entire life was one continuous "yes" to the will of God.

Recall that at the wedding feast of Cana, water was turned into wine through Mary's intercession with her son. She told the servants at the wedding: "Do whatever he tells you." Her role has not changed. She continues to intercede and she continues to point to her Son.

St. Louis Marie de Montfort and St. Maximilian Kolbe are foremost in the promotion of this practice of consecration to Mary. Both emphasize that this devotion to Mary is not an end in itself but rather a means to become more dedicated to the service of Christ. They point out that there is no surer way to Jesus than through His mother. There are various practices that are encouraged for those who choose consecration to the Blessed Mother — the consecration prayer, daily Rosary, etc. However, both saints point out that more important than external observances is the inner disposition of the person. Montfort identifies four facets of the inner disposition. First the Marian devotee is to be open to the Holy Spirit's activity through Mary. He/she is to develop a familiarity with the mind of Mary and to be of one mind with Mary, who is the model. Also Montfort counsels the individual to be conscious that he or she rests in the maternal care of Mary. Finally the saint encourages dedication of self in total commitment to the service of Mary.

Pope John Paul II has encouraged the approach of St. Louis Marie de Montfort as both appropriate and helpful for the Catholic. The Holy Father has consecrated himself to Mary according to Montfort's approach. A fuller explanation of Consecration to Mary can be found in Montfort's book *True Devotion to the Blessed Virgin*.

Hold That Thought

It was mentioned at the beginning of this chapter that the word "consecration" is not understood by many in our society. Also using the word "consecration" in reference to Mary can be problematic. A proper understanding of the term is provided in the works of St. Louis Marie de Montfort and St. Maximilian Kolbe. Nonetheless, to avoid confusion among the faithful, Pope John Paul II has moved away from the use of the word "consecration" in reference to Mary. Instead the Holy Father uses the word "entrustment." This may be a term more readily understandable to people in our society.

"Mary said, 'Behold, I am the handmaid of the Lord. May it be done to me according to your word.' "

— Luke 1:38 (NAB)

(Note: This was Mary's willing consecration of her life to the will of God.)

Consecrated to Christ

"In Baptism . . . he [the Christian] has taken Jesus Christ for his Master and Sovereign Lord, to depend on Him in the quality of a slave of love. That is what we do by this present devotion."

— St. Louis Marie de Montfort

" . . . At one point I began to question any devotion to Mary, believing that, if it became too great, it might end up compromising the supremacy of the worship owed Christ. At that time, I was greatly helped by a book by St. Louis Marie Grignion de Montfort entitled *True Devotion to the Blessed Virgin*. There I found the answers to my questions. Yes, Mary does bring us closer to Christ; she does lead us to Him, provided that we live her mystery in Christ. . . . Thanks to St. Louis, I began to discover the immense riches of Marian devotion from new perspectives."

— Pope John Paul II

"[Apostles of these latter times] will know the grandeurs of the Queen, and will consecrate themselves entirely to her service as subjects and slaves of love. They shall be true apostles of the latter times."

— St. Louis Marie de Montfort

The Promises of Our Lord
to St. Margaret Mary

For Souls Devoted to His Sacred Heart

1. "I will give them all the graces necessary in their state of life."

2. "I will establish peace in their homes."

3. "I will comfort them in all their afflictions."

4. "I will be their secure refuge during life, and above all in death."

5. "I will bestow a large blessing upon all their undertakings."

6. "Sinners shall find in My Heart the source and the infinite ocean of mercy."

7. "Tepid souls shall grow fervent."

8. "Fervent souls shall quickly mount to high perfection."

9. "I will bless every place where a picture of My Heart shall be set up and honored."

10. "I will give to priests the gifts of touching the most hardened hearts."

11. "Those who shall promote this devotion shall have their names written in My Heart, never to be effaced."

12. "I promise you in the excessive mercy of My Heart that My all-powerful love will grant to all those who communicate on the First Friday in nine consecutive months the grace of final penitence; they shall not die in My disgrace nor without receiving their sacraments; My divine Heart shall be their safe refuge in this last moment."

Prayers

Consecration of the Family to the Sacred Heart of Jesus

Sacred Heart of Jesus, You made clear to St. Margaret Mary Your desire of being King in Christian families. We today wish to proclaim Your most complete kingly dominion over our own family. We want to live in the future with Your life. We want to cause to flourish in our midst those virtues to which You have promised peace here below. We want to banish far from us the spirit of the world, which You have cursed. You shall be King over our minds in the simplicity of our faith, and over our hearts by the wholehearted love with which they shall burn for You, the flame of which we will keep alive by the frequent reception of Your divine Eucharist. Be so kind, O divine Heart, as to preside over our assemblings, to bless our enterprises, both spiritual and temporal, to dispel our cares, to sanctify our joys, and to alleviate our sufferings. If ever one or other of us should have the misfortune to afflict You, remind him, O Heart of Jesus, that You are good and merciful to the penitent sinner. And when the hour of separation strikes, when death shall come to cast mourning into our midst, we will all, both those who go and those who stay, be submissive to Your eternal decrees. We shall console ourselves with the thought that a day will come when the entire family, reunited in heaven, can sing forever Your glories and Your mercies. May the Immaculate Heart of Mary and the glorious patriarch St. Joseph present this consecration to You, and keep it in our minds all the days of our life. All glory to the Heart of Jesus, our King and our Father!

— From *My Catholic Devotions*

Consecration to the
Sacred Heart of Jesus

Adorable Heart of Jesus, the most tender, the most amiable, the most generous of all hearts, penetrated with gratitude at the sight of Your benefits, I come to consecrate myself wholly and unreservedly to You! I wish to devote all my energies to propagating Your worship and winning, if possible, all hearts to You. Receive my heart this day, O Jesus! Or rather take it, change it, purify it, to render it worthy of You; make it humble, gentle, patient, faithful, and generous like Your heart, by inflaming it with the fire of Your love. Hide it in Your Divine Heart with all hearts that love You and are consecrated to You; never permit me to take my heart from You again. Let me rather die than grieve Your Adorable Heart. You know O Heart of Jesus, that the desire of my heart is to love You always, to be wholly Yours in life and in death, in time and in eternity. Most Sacred Heart of Jesus, have mercy on us. Sacred Heart of Jesus, I trust in You.

— St. Margaret Mary Alacoque

Consecration to the
Immaculate Heart of Mary

I, *(your name)*, a faithless sinner, renew and ratify today in your hands, O Immaculate Mother, the vows of my Baptism; I renounce Satan, his pomps and works; and I give myself entirely to Jesus Christ, the Incarnate Wisdom, to carry my cross after Him all the days of my life, and to be more faithful to Him than I have ever been before. In the presence of all the Heavenly court I choose you this day for my Mother and Mistress. I deliver and consecrate to you, as your slave, my body and soul, my goods, both interior and exterior, and even the value of all my good actions, past, present, and future; leaving to you the entire and full right of disposing of me, and all that belongs to me, without exception, according to thy good pleasure, for the greater glory of God, in time and in eternity. Amen.

— St. Louis de Montfort

Daily Renewal of Total Consecration

Immaculata, Queen and Mother of the Church, I renew my consecration to you for this day and for always, so that you might use me for the coming of the Kingdom of Jesus in the whole world. To this end I offer you all my prayers, actions, and sacrifices of this day.

— St. Maximilian Kolbe

Consecration Prayer for Children to Jesus

Dear Sacred Heart of Jesus, I love You so much and I give You my heart. Help me to love God. Help me to love my neighbor as a child of God. Help me to love myself as a child of God. Amen.

Consecration Prayer for Children to Mary

Dear Mary, my Holy Mother, I love you so much and I give you my heart. Help me to love God. Help me to love my neighbor as a child of God. Help me to love myself as a child of God. Amen.

How to Make a Pilgrimage to a Holy Place

Whether the journey is to Jerusalem or to an outdoor shrine that is a mile from your home, a pilgrimage can draw you closer to Our Lord.

More than a physical journey, a pilgrimage is a spiritual journey. The word pilgrim is derived from a Latin word that means "stranger." Where you live may be scenic and pleasant, but it is not your home! Our citizenship is in heaven with Christ (Phil 3:20). "Here we have no lasting city, but we seek the city which is to come" (Heb 13:14).

Now we are not wanderers; we are pilgrims. We know where we started from, and we are headed to a new land. Our sojourn is purposeful; it has meaning and direction. We even have a guide on the route — the Holy Spirit working through the Church

The concept of pilgrimage is biblical. The Israelites, directed by God, left Egypt and set out for the Promised Land. They took only what they could carry for the journey for their trust was in God. The Ark of the Covenant, the sign of God's presence with His people in the Old Testament, was carried by the Levites as the people journeyed.

After the building of the temple, the Israelites would make a pilgrimage to the temple to worship God. Yearly, devout Jews celebrate that going forth and renew their trust in God and in His provision. We can recall the journey that Mary, Joseph, and Jesus made from Nazareth to Jerusalem, and Jesus remaining in the temple until found again by His parents.

Psalms 120 through 134 are called "Songs of Ascents" because they were sung as pilgrims made their trip to Jerusalem. Their themes vary, but the longing to be close to the Lord unites them.

Christian pilgrimages have a long and glorious history. Perhaps the most famous pilgrim is St. Helen, the mother of the Emperor Constantine. Helen traveled to the Holy Land and there discovered the true cross of Jesus. Many followed her example and made the journey to the Holy Land. However, the locations of the life and death of Jesus were not the only destinations for pilgrims. The burial place of saints, especially of martyrs, and various shrines dedicated to the Blessed Mother were favorite destinations for the pilgrim.

Christian pilgrims resembled their Jewish forbears in many ways. Like the ancient Israelites, they made their journey usually in groups. No longer was the Ark of the Covenant the sign of God's presence. Instead, the Catholic pilgrims carried and often wore a cross. Like the Israelites on their journey to the Promised Land, these pilgrims traveled simply. They wore simple garb and traveled with a minimum of provisions. Normally they walked. The medieval pilgrims added their own hymns to the Virgin and the Savior to the standard Psalms from the Old Testament.

The reasons for a pilgrimage varied. Some people made the journey to do penance. It may have been assigned by a confessor or done voluntarily. Others made the pilgrimage as a thanksgiving to God for some specific favor or in general thanksgiving. Still others made the journey to focus their energies on drawing closer to God — the physical journey was a sign of their commitment to the spiritual journey.

How does the Catholic of today take part in this tradition of pilgrimage? It is still a pious practice to make a prayerful journey to the historic sites: Jerusalem, Rome, Lourdes, Fátima, etc. However, it is also possible to take advantage of the spirit of a pilgrimage in your own city or town. First, identify a church or shrine. As did the medieval pilgrims, you may wish to travel with someone else or in a small group. Drive or walk to the destination of your pilgrimage and proceed with an attitude of prayer. One approach is to plan to say the entire fifteen decades of the Rosary — "traveling" with Jesus through the mysteries. Say the Joyful Mysteries on the way to the pilgrimage site. Say the Sorrowful Mysteries at the church or shrine. On the return trip pray the Glorious Mysteries. Other prayers can be used, but the Rosary provides a convenient format for the traveling pilgrim.

There are certain seasons of the liturgical year that lend themselves to pilgrimage. Lent is a time that we focus on repentance as we journey toward Easter. Your destination could be an area church where you pray the Stations of the Cross. At Christmas time you can imitate the example of the Magi and make a pilgrimage to a specific manger scene. During May, the month of Mary, a trip to a Marian shrine or Church in your diocese would be appropriate.

It's useful to distinguish between making a pilgrimage and going on a tour — although once the pilgrimage is over many people also tour. A pilgrimage is a very deliberate act, a setting out in order to draw closer to God. A tour may edify us, teach us, and give us time to relax in new things, but it is not a pilgrimage.

The distinction used to be easier to make because in the past traveling was more uncertain. To take days and weeks to go someplace specific to worship God used to be a larger sacrifice, and in the developing world it still is. In the developing world now, and all over the world in the past, travelers could not presume they would make their destination. Bandits, disease, weariness, unreliable transportation, wars, all could interfere. It's useful to remember this when setting out on a modern-day pilgrimage which, in comparison, can seem little more than a vacation.

Consider This

A pilgrimage can be a wonderful family event. The family can pick an area church or outdoor shrine and make the pilgrimage on a Sunday afternoon as both a family event and a means of keeping the sabbath holy. Children can take an active role in the prayers. You can take flowers to place at the shrine or in front of a statue at the church. Lighting a candle at the church while praying for a particular intention adds solemnity to the event. Also, when the family takes a vacation to a different city or area of the county, plan to make a small pilgrimage as part of the vacation. It teaches the children that love of Jesus takes priority in the family life.

The crusades were an outgrowth of the medieval approach to pilgrimages to the Holy Land. The goal of the crusades was to free the sacred places in the Holy Land from the control of the Muslims. Today some pro-life Catholics have begun a practice, that may be called a spiritual crusade. They attend Mass as a group and then travel to an abortion clinic. During the journey, they maintain a prayerful attitude, perhaps saying the Rosary or singing hymns. They quietly gather near the abortion clinic and spend a designated time in reverent prayer. This harkens back to the practice of making a pilgrimage in reparation for sin. In this instance the pilgrimage and prayers are offered in reparation for the sin of abortion. It is a prayer crusade for the men and women who are victimized by abortion and for the children who are killed in the clinics.

We Are But Travelers

"Our home is — Heaven. On earth we are like travelers staying in a hotel. When one is away, one is always thinking of going home."

— St. John Vianney

"Without the Way, there is no going; without the Truth, there is no knowing; without the Life, there is no living."

— From *The Imitation of Christ*, Thomas à Kempis

"We are but travelers on a journey without as yet a fixed abode; we are on our way, not yet in our native land; we are in a state of longing, but not yet of enjoyment. But let us continue on our way, and continue without sloth or respite, so that we may ultimately arrive at our destination."

— St. Augustine

Prayer for Automobile Travel

Lord God, be well-disposed to our prayers, and bless this vehicle with Your holy hand. Appoint Your holy angels as an escort over it, who will always shield its passengers and keep them safe from accidents. And as once by Your deacon, Philip, You bestowed faith and grace upon the Ethiopian seated in his carriage and reading Holy Scripture, so also now show the way of salvation to Your servants, in order that, strengthened by Your grace and ever intent upon good works, they may attain, after all the successes and failures of this life, the certain happiness of everlasting life; through Christ Our Lord. Amen.

— From *Prayers and Blessings for Daily Life in Christ*

How to Pray a Novena

Before Jesus ascended into heaven He directed His disciples to remain in Jerusalem and "wait for the promise of the Father" (Acts 1:4). His disciples, along with Mary, His Mother, waited in the upper room and here they "devoted themselves to prayer" (Acts 1:14). Nine days later they realized the "promise of the Father" as the Holy Spirit came upon them, empowering them to proclaim the Good News.

This is the model for the many novenas that have developed over the ages. Novena means "nine days." Novenas are private, personal devotions rather than "official" liturgical devotions. They date back to Roman times. The first novenas were nine days of Masses and prayers for the soul of the deceased. The novena was prayed in particular at the death of a pope or cardinal. This type of novena may have arisen because Scripture says that Jesus died at the "ninth" hour.

Parallel to the novena for the departed, the novena of preparation also developed. Again it consisted of nine days of prayer. These prayers anticipated a feast and had the goal of preparing the Catholic to enter fully into the feast. The first such novena was celebrated during the nine days prior to Christmas. In addition to the special prayers, nine votive Masses were said in honor of the Blessed Mother.

In the seventeenth century many religious orders began the practice of celebrating a novena in preparation for the feast of their founder. This devotion spread in popularity among the faithful. Thus, the nine days before important liturgical feasts were commemorated with special prayers and Masses of preparation.

A further development found the faithful offering novena prayers to specific saints for particular needs. Rather than a novena of preparation, these were novenas of prayers for particular needs and could occur at anytime during the year. Many who suffered from illness or had specific needs would pray for nine consecutive days and ask the intercession of a saint for healing or assistance.

Most novenas consist of a novena prayer that is repeated daily. Additionally, on each of the nine days there are specific prayers and reflections for the particular day. Reception of the sacraments of confession and Communion often are incorporated in the nine-day devotion.

Novenas are almost too many and varied to enumerate. However, there are some novenas that have been more popular than others. There is a novena to the Holy Trinity, which is made prior to the feast of the Holy Trinity (the Sunday after Pentecost). There are several novenas to the Holy Spirit which can be made prior to the feast of Pentecost and mirror that proto-novena which was prayed by Mary and the disciples in Jerusalem. There are novenas for use prior to Christmas. Novenas to the Sacred Heart of Jesus have been popular and can be prayed in anticipation of the feast. There are at least eleven novenas to the Blessed Mother. The most popular may be the one prior to the feast of the Immaculate Conception. The novena that anticipates the feast of St. Joseph on March 19 honors the foster father of Jesus.

Additionally there are many novenas to saints and angels that may or may not anticipate a particular feast. Some of these include St. Jude, St. Francis Xavier, St. Thérèse of the Little Flower, and St. Anne.

A novena of recent development comes from the "Divine Mercy" devotion. On Good Friday, 1937, a Polish nun, Sister Faustina, sensed that Jesus was requesting that a novena be prayed in anticipation of the Sunday after Easter. Specific prayers brought different groups of souls each day before the Lord of Mercy for special graces.

Novena prayers are available from Catholic bookstores or from various apostolates. Most come with their own particular instructions.

Novena Prayers

Novena Prayer to St. Joseph

St. Joseph, I, your unworthy child, greet you. You are the faithful protector and intercessor of all who love and venerate you. You know that I have special confidence in you and that, after Jesus and Mary, I place all my hope of salvation in you, for you are especially powerful with God and will never abandon your faithful servants. Therefore I humbly invoke you and commend myself, with all who are dear to me and all that belong to me, to your intercession. I beg of you, by your love for Jesus and Mary, not to abandon me during life and to assist me at the hour of my death.

Glorious St. Joseph, spouse of the Immaculate Virgin, obtain for me a pure, humble, charitable mind, and perfect resignation to the divine will. Be my guide, my father, and my model through life that I may merit to die as you did in the arms of Jesus and Mary.

Loving St. Joseph, faithful follower of Jesus Christ, I raise my heart to you to implore your powerful intercession in obtaining from the Divine Heart of Jesus all the graces necessary for my spiritual and temporal welfare, particularly the grace of a happy death, and the special grace I now implore: *(Mention your request here)*.

Guardian of the Word Incarnate, I feel confident that your prayers in my behalf will be graciously heard before the throne of God. Amen.

Prayers for the Fifth Day of the Novena to the Divine Mercy

For the souls of those who have separated themselves from my church

Most Merciful Jesus, Goodness Itself, You do not refuse light to those who seek it of You. Receive into the abode of Your Most Compassionate Heart the souls of those who have separated themselves from Your Church. Draw them by Your light into the unity of the Church, and do not let them escape from the abode of Your Most Compassionate Heart; but bring it about that they, too, come to glorify the generosity of Your mercy.

Eternal Father, turn Your merciful gaze upon the souls of those who have separated themselves from Your Son's Church, who have squandered Your blessings and misused Your graces by obstinately persisting in their errors. Do not look upon their errors, but upon the love of Your own Son and upon His bitter Passion, which He underwent for their sake, since they, too, are enclosed in His Most Compassionate Heart. Bring it about that they also may glorify Your great mercy for endless ages. Amen.

— "The Divine Mercy Message and Devotions,"
by Marians of the Immaculate Conception
(copyright 1995)

Novena Prayer to the Holy Spirit

(In anticipation of the feast of Pentecost)

O Holy Spirit, O my God, I adore You, and acknowledge, here in Your divine presence, that I am nothing and can do nothing without You. Come, great Paraclete, father of the poor, comforter the best, fulfill the promise of our blessed Savior, Who would not leave us orphans, and come into the mind and the heart of your poor, unworthy creature, as You did descend on the sacred day of Pentecost on the holy Mother of Jesus and on His first disciples. Grant that I may participate in those gifts, which You did communicate to them so wonderfully, and with so much mercy and generosity. Take from my heart whatever is not pleasing to You, and make of it a worthy dwelling-place for Yourself. Illumine my mind, that I may see and understand the things that are for my eternal good. Inflame my heart with pure love of You, that I may be cleansed from the dross of all inordinate attachments, and that my whole life may be hidden with Jesus in God. Strengthen my will, that I may be made conformable to Your divine will, and be guided by Your holy inspirations. Aid me by Your grace to practice the divine lessons of humility, poverty, obedience, and contempt of the world, which Jesus taught us in His mortal life. Oh, rend the heavens, and come down, consoling Spirit! That inspired and encouraged by You, I may faithfully comply with the duties of my state, carry my daily cross most patiently, and endeavor to accomplish the divine will with the utmost perfection. Spirit of love! Spirit of purity! Spirit of peace! Sanctify my soul more and more, and give me that heavenly peace which the world cannot give. Bless our Holy Father the Pope, bless the Church, bless our bishops, our priests, all Religious Orders, and all the faithful, that they may be filled with the spirit of Christ and labor earnestly for the spread of His kingdom. O Holy Spirit, Giver of every good and perfect gift, grant me, I beseech You, the intentions of this novena. May Your will be done in me and through me. May You be praised and glorified forevermore!

Exaltation of the Holy Cross Novena

Jesus, Who because of Your burning love for us willed to be crucified and to shed Your Most Precious Blood for the redemption and salvation of our souls, look down upon us and grant the petition we ask for. . . .

We trust completely in Your Mercy. Cleanse us from sin by Your Grace, sanctify our work, give us and all those who are dear to us our daily bread, lighten the burden of our sufferings, bless our families, and grant to the nations, so sorely afflicted, Your Peace, which is the only true peace, so that by obeying Your Commandments we may come at last to the glory of Heaven.

Novena Prayer
to the Immaculate Heart of Mary

O Most Blessed Mother, heart of love, heart of mercy, ever listening, caring, consoling, hear our prayer. As your children, we implore your intercession with Jesus your Son. Receive with understanding and compassion the petitions we place before you today, especially *(mention your request here)*.

We are comforted in knowing your heart is ever open to those who ask for your prayer. We trust to your gentle care and intercession, those whom we love and who are sick or lonely or hurting. Help all of us, Holy Mother, to bear our burdens in this life until we may share eternal life and peace with God forever. Amen.

How to Pray
the Stations of the Cross

In almost every Catholic church you can find four-teen images marked by a cross on the walls. These images trace Jesus' journey from the trial before Pilate to His crucifixion and death on Calvary. This series is called the "Stations" or "Way" of the Cross.

Traditionally, pilgrims to Jerusalem would follow the route of Jesus' Passion, stopping along the way to meditate on various events. The practice of praying the Stations of the Cross allows us to imitate those pilgrims and to meditate on our Lord's Passion and death.

Pope John Paul II has, for his own devotions, modified the more traditional versions. The numbering of his Stations are slightly different and focus on fourteen events mentioned in the Scriptures.

No matter which version you choose, you may pray the Stations anywhere — at church or at home. And you can pray them by yourself or with a group. Many churches celebrate the communal prayer of the Stations on Fridays during Lent.

The normal procedure is to walk from station to station — as it were, walking the Passion with Jesus. At each station, stop and reflect on the aspect of the Passion represented on the particular image. A devotional text can be used to assist in meditation. Or you may meditate and pray in your own words.

It is customary to begin each Station by praying: "We adore You, O Christ, and we praise You; because by Your Holy Cross You have redeemed the world." It is customary to genuflect while reciting this prayer. The meditation will follow. Often the meditation ends with the recitation of the Our Father, Hail Mary, and Glory Be. Before moving to the next Station, some will pray: "Have mercy on us, O Lord; have mercy on us."

Although the above is customary and helpful for many, it is not necessary. What is required in the devotion is the "walk" through each event with pause for meditation. The

"walk" does not need to be an actual physical walk. It is quite possible to pray the stations while sitting in a chair — calling to mind each station, perhaps with the aid of a booklet with pictures.

The practice of "walking the Passion with Jesus" is quite ancient. However it became a popular devotion throughout Europe during the Middle Ages. The Franciscan preachers in particular encouraged the devotion.

Since our Lord's Passion and death are the source of endless depth of meaning, this is a devotion that never ages. The meditations offered in Catholic literature are many and varied. Below are some samples. Written

mediations on the Way of the Cross can be purchased at Catholic bookstores or even acquired "online" on the Internet.

Prayers and Meditations

Preparatory Prayer

(MEDITATION BY ST. ALPHONSUS LIGUORI)

My Lord Jesus, You have made this journey to die for me with love unutterable, and I have so many times unworthily abandoned You; but now I love You with my whole heart, and because I love You, I repent sincerely for ever having offended You. Pardon me, my God, and permit me to accompany You on this journey. You go to die for love of me; I wish also, my beloved Redeemer, to die for love of You. My Jesus, I will live and die united to You.

The First Station:
Jesus Is Condemned to Death

(MEDITATION BY ST. ALPHONSUS LIGUORI)

Consider that Jesus, after having been scourged and crowned with thorns, was unjustly condemned by Pilate to die on the cross.

My adorable Jesus, it was not Pilate, no, it was my sins, that condemned You to die. I beseech You, by the merits of this sorrowful journey, to assist my soul in its journey towards eternity. I love You, my beloved Jesus; I love You more than myself; I repent with my whole heart of having offended You. Never permit me to separate myself from You again. Grant that I may love You always, and then do with me what You will.

The Second Station: Jesus is made to carry the cross
The Third Station: Jesus falls the first time

The Fourth Station:
Jesus Meets His Sorrowful Mother
(MEDITATION BY BLESSED JOSÉMARIA ESCRIVÁ)

No sooner has Jesus risen from His first fall than He meets His Blessed Mother, standing by the wayside where He is passing.

With immense love Mary looks at Jesus, and Jesus at His mother. Their eyes meet, and each heart pours into the other its own deep sorrow. Mary's soul is steeped in the bitter grief, the grief of Jesus Christ.

"O all you that pass by the way, look and see, was there ever a sorrow to compare with my sorrow!" (Lm 1:12).

But no one notices, no one pays attention; only Jesus.

Simeon's prophecy has been fulfilled: "thine own soul a sword shall pierce" (Lk 2:35).

In the dark loneliness of the Passion, our Lady offers her Son a comforting balm of tenderness, of union, of faithfulness; a "yes" to the divine will.

Hand in hand with Mary, you and I also want to console Jesus, by accepting always and in everything the will of His Father, of our Father.

Only thus will we taste the sweetness of Christ's cross and come to embrace it with all the strength of Love, carrying it in triumph along the ways of the earth.

The Fifth Station:
Simon of Cyrene Helps Jesus to Carry the Cross
(MEDITATION BY CARDINAL NEWMAN)

Jesus could bear His Cross alone, did He so will; but He permits Simon to help Him, in order to remind us that we must take part in His sufferings, and have a fellowship in His work. His merit is infinite, yet He condescends to let His people add their merit to it. The sanctity of the Blessed Virgin, the blood of the Martyrs, the prayers and penances of the Saints, the good deeds of all the faithful, take part in that work which, nevertheless, is perfect without them. He saves us by His blood, but it is through and with ourselves that He saves us. Dear Lord, teach us to suffer with You, make it pleasant to us to suffer for Your sake, and sanctify all our sufferings by the merits of Your own.

The Sixth Station: Veronica wipes the face of Jesus
The Seventh Station: Jesus falls the second time
The Eighth Station: Jesus speaks to the women

The Ninth: Jesus Falls the Third Time
(MEDITATION BY REV. JAMES ALBERIONE, S.S.P.)

Jesus falls the third time beneath the cross to teach us not to be obstinate. Obstinacy can lead us to sin again.

O Jesus, grant me the grace to be faithful to my resolutions.

The Tenth Station: Jesus is stripped of His garments

The Eleventh Station:
Jesus Is Nailed to the Cross
(MEDITATION BY CARDINAL NEWMAN)

Jesus is pierced through each hand and each foot with a sharp nail. His eyes are dimmed with blood, and are closed by the swollen lids and livid brows, which the blows of His executioners have caused. His mouth is filled with vinegar and gall. His head is encircled by the sharp thorns. His heart is pierced with the spear. Thus, all His senses are mortified and crucified, that He may make atonement for every kind of human sin. O Jesus, mortify and crucify us with You. Let us never sin by hand or foot, by eyes or mouth, or by head or heart. Let all our senses be a sacrifice to You; let every member sing Your praise. Let the sacred blood which flowed from Thy five wounds anoint us with such sanctifying grace that we may die to the world, and live only to Thee.

The Twelfth: Jesus Dies on the Cross
(MEDITATION BY ST. FRANCIS OF ASSISI)

Behold Jesus crucified! Behold His wounds, received for love of you! His whole appearance betokens love: His head is bent to kiss you; His arms are extended to embrace you; His heart is open to receive you. O superabundant love, Jesus, the Son of God, dies upon the cross, that man may live and be delivered from everlasting death!

O most amiable Jesus! Who will grant me that I may die for You! I will at least endeavor to die to the world. How must I regard the world and its vanities, when I behold You hanging on the cross, covered with wounds? O Jesus receive me into Your wounded heart: I belong entirely to You; for You alone do I desire to live and to die.

The Thirteenth Station: Jesus is taken down from the cross and placed in the arms of His Mother

The Fourteenth Station: Jesus is laid in the tomb

Concluding Prayer

(According to St. Francis of Assisi)

Almighty and eternal God, merciful Father, Who has given to the human race Your beloved Son as an example of humility, obedience, and patience, to precede us on the way of life, bearing the cross: Graciously grant us that we, inflamed by His infinite love, may take up the sweet yoke of His Gospel together with the mortification of the cross, following Him as His true disciples, so that we shall one day gloriously rise with Him and joyfully hear the final sentence: "Come, you blessed of My Father, and possess the kingdom which was prepared for you from the beginning." Where You reign with the Son and the Holy Spirit, and where we hope to reign with You, world without end. Amen.

Pope John Paul II's
Stations of the Cross

THE FIRST STATION: Jesus' agony in the garden

THE SECOND STATION: Jesus is betrayed by Judas and is arrested

THE THIRD STATION: Jesus is condemned by the Sanhedrin

THE FOURTH STATION: Jesus is denied by Peter

THE FIFTH STATION: Jesus is condemned by Pontius Pilate

THE SIXTH STATION: Jesus is scourged and crowned with thorns

THE SEVENTH STATION: Jesus is made to carry the cross

THE EIGHTH STATION: Simon of Cyrene helps Jesus carry His cross

THE NINTH STATION: Jesus meets with the women of Jerusalem

THE TENTH STATION: Jesus is nailed to the Cross

THE ELEVENTH STATION: Jesus promises paradise to the repentant thief

THE TWELFTH STATION: Jesus speaks to John and Mary on the cross

THE THIRTEENTH STATION: Jesus dies on the cross

THE FOURTEENTH STATION: Jesus is laid in the tomb

How to Use Holy Water

Holy water is just one of the Church's many sacramentals. A sacramental is any action or object blessed by the Church to inspire Christians to prayer and the love of God. Sacramentals prepare the heart and mind to be more open to grace.

Holy Water is a sacramental that points to the Sacrament of Baptism. In Baptism, we are cleansed of sin, incorporated into Christ, filled with sanctifying grace, and given gifts of the Holy Spirit. When we use holy water, we are recalling our Baptism and the action of God in that sacrament.

The concept of holy water has its roots in the Old Testament. Water was used by the Levitical priests in blessing of objects of worship and sacrifice. It was also used to sprinkle the repentant sinner and those seeking cleansing from various ritual impurities.

The present blessing of holy water focuses on the connection to Baptism and asks that the person who uses the water would receive help in remaining "faithful to the sacrament received in faith." Therefore when we use holy water, we should recall our Baptism. By making the Sign of the Cross with the water on our fingers, we recall the Trinitarian formula of our Baptism. In addition to reflecting on the grace we receive in the Sacrament of Initiation, we can consciously ask Our Lord to continue to grant us graces to live out our baptismal promises.

Consider This

After Vatican Council II the various blessings associated with sacramentals were revised. The official English translation of these blessings was promulgated in 1988. The revised blessing of holy water focuses on the connection to Baptism — holy water is meant to "reconnect" us to the grace and life that we received in that sacrament.

Prior blessings for holy water included a number of intercessions that have now been omitted. For example, the previous rite included the intercession: "O God . . . grant that this creature of Thine (water) may be endowed with divine grace to drive away devils and to cast out diseases, that whatever in the houses or possessions of the faithful may be sprinkled by this water, so that health which they seek by calling upon Thy Holy Name may be guarded from all assaults."

The intercessions offered at the blessing of the water were part and parcel of the use of the water. In fact, in the old blessing, the priest would end the intercessions: "If they use it, God grant them all these things."

Based on the blessings, many people would use holy water in family devotions when they invoked God's protection on their family or prayed for the healing of a family member who was sick or troubled. Was and is that use of holy water invalid based on the change in the blessing since 1988? The answer is a simple "no." In fact the Church still uses holy water in the rite of exorcism (casting out a demon) and in the blessings of various objects and of various people including those in difficulty or experiencing trials (e.g., "Order of Blessing of Parents after a Miscarriage").

It was and is possible to treat holy water, or any sacramental, in a superstitious way by viewing the sacramental as the source of some "magical" cure or protection. In actuality it is the prayer of the church, the grace of the sacraments, the action of God, and the disposition and prayers of the person who uses the sacramental which are the effective elements. By way of example, consider a bank check. In itself the check has no value — it is only a piece of paper. However, the money in the bank associated with that checking account and the endorsement of the account holder give value. The parallel is not perfect, but it does show that the value can be derived from another source.

In Baptism we become children of God and members of the Church. As God's children we enjoy His love and protection. Christ does drive away Satan. God Who is concerned about every aspect of our lives, does bring forgiveness, healing, and strength.

When we pray for people who are sick and sprinkle that person with holy water, is it the holy water that works a cure? Certainly it is God and His grace that accomplish the healing.

Thus holy water is still very useful in family devotions. Many parents will sprinkle holy water on their children as they pray for God's protection upon them. This action joins the prayers of the parents with the action and prayers of the Church and provides a tangible sign of the blessing we have as children of God.

In addition, parents have a "priestly" role in the home to teach, guide, and pray for their children. The use of holy water assists parents in this function. It also connects the prayers and actions of the domestic church (the family) with the prayers and actions of the Universal Church.

Sacred Signs

"And the priest shall take holy water in an earthen vessel and take some of the dust that is on the floor of the tabernacle and put it into the water."

— **Numbers 5:17**

"From long experience I have learned that there is nothing like holy water to put devils to flight."

— **St. Teresa of Ávila**

". . . Whenever I take [holy water], my soul feels a particular and most notable consolation. In fact, it is quite usual for me to be conscious of a refreshment, which I cannot possibly describe, resembling an inward joy, which comforts my whole soul. This is not fancy, or something, which has happened to me only once; it has happened again and again and I have observed it most attentively. It is, let us say, as if someone very hot and thirsty were to drink from a jug of cold water: he would feel the refreshment throughout his body. I often reflect on the great importance of everything ordained by the Church and it makes me very happy to find that those words of the Church are so powerful that they impart their power to the water and make it so very different from water which has not been blessed."

— **St. Teresa of Ávila**

"Blessed are You, Lord, all powerful God, Who in Christ, the living water of salvation, blessed and transformed us. Grant that, when we are sprinkled with this water or make use of it, we will be refreshed inwardly by the power of the Holy Spirit and continue to walk in the new life we received at Baptism."

— **Excerpt from
"Order for the Blessing of Holy Water"**

How to Use a Vigil Candle

Light and fire are rich symbols in the Bible and in Church life. The first chapter of the Gospel of John refers to Christ as the light of the world. At Baptism we receive a lighted candle as the priest or deacon says: "Receive the Light of Christ." Jesus tells us that we are to show forth His light to the world and not to keep it "hidden under a basket" (Mt 5:15).

Candles have long been used at Mass and at the funeral and burial of Catholics. During the Easter season, the large Paschal candle burns in the Church to proclaim that Christ is risen from the dead.

Packing such symbolic power, lighting candles has always been among the most popular Catholic devotional practices. In many churches, chapels, and shrines, there are designated areas where the faithful can light a candle that is set before a sacred image. These candles are often called "vigil lights."

After lighting a candle, you should offer a prayer. Your prayer may thank God for a favor or blessing. Or you may thank a particular saint for intercession for your special need. Or you may bring a petition to Our Lord, His mother, or one of the saints. Depending on its size and environmental conditions, the candle you've lit may burn for a few hours or as long as a week. It is customary to leave a small monetary offering at the chapel, at least enough to cover the cost of the candle; in some cases the donation is specified.

The lit candle visualizes your prayer. The candle then "keeps vigil" in the church or shrine when you cannot physically be present. Meanwhile, though you travel far from the place of worship, you should continue your prayers.

Your lighted candle joins with those left by others as

a tangible sign of the combined prayers of the community. Many small lights make for a greater cumulative brilliance. When you see those flames you can offer a prayer for all the needs that they represent in your community of faith.

Hold That Thought

The use of candles in churches and at shrines did not originate with the Church. In ancient times the practice was well known in pagan religions. However, in the Catholic Church this practice took on a new meaning, for we know Jesus Christ, the true Light, Who shines in the darkness.

Light a Candle

"Lights are kindled, though the sun is already shining, not indeed to dispel darkness, but to exhibit a token of joy."

— St. Jerome

"Lights are burnt, odorous with waxed papyri. They shine by night and day; thus night is radiant with the brightness of the day, and the day itself, bright in heavenly beauty, shines yet more with light doubled by countless lamps."

— St. Paulinus of Nola

"No one who lights a lamp conceals it with a vessel or sets it under a bed; rather, he places it on a lampstand so that those who enter may see the light."

— Luke 8:16 (NAB)

How to Wear a Scapular

A scapular is another one of the Church's sacramentals. The name comes from the Latin word, *scapula*, which means "shoulder." Originally a scapular was a garment worn only by members of a religious order. It was worn over the head and rested on the shoulders and normally hung almost to the feet. Many religious still wear a similar type of scapular as a sign of their profession. The scapular is to the religious what the "stole" is to a priest — a sign of the priestly dignity and office.

The sixteenth century was the time of the Catholic Reformation. It was a time of growth of religious orders and of popular devotion. Many Catholics wished to be associated with the great religious orders such as the Benedictines and Carmelites, the Franciscans and Dominicans. Lay people who were not able to join the order nonetheless wished to participate in the spirituality of the order. The response was the establishment of "third" orders and lay movements attached to particular religious communities. The faithful would be formally installed into the order's life by a simple investiture service. During the service a modified scapular was placed on the shoulders of the new conferee as a sign of affiliation. The scapular represented both the commitment to live the spirituality of the order as well as the opportunity to participate in its prayers and blessings.

The scapular for the laity was designed to be worn easily in their daily life, often underneath the clothing. Yet the wearing of the scapular served as a continuing reminder and sign of the individual's commitment to the spirituality it represented.

There are at least eighteen different scapulars approved by the Church for popular devotion. Some of these are associated with religious orders, while others are associated with lay apostolates and movements.

Various Types of Scapulars

- of Mount Carmel, the so-called "brown scapular"
- of the Hearts of Jesus and Mary, white
- of the help of the sick, black
- of the Holy Face, white
- of the Immaculate Conception, blue
- of the Immaculate Heart of Mary, white surmounted on green, hence known as the "green scapular"
- of the Mother of Good Counsel, white
- of Our Lady of Ransom, the white of the Mercedarian Order
- of the Passion, red
- of the Passion, the black scapular of the Passionist Congregation
- of the Precious Blood, red
- of the Sacred Heart of Jesus, also referred to as the Badge of the Sacred Heart, red
- of St. Benedict, black
- of St. Dominic, white
- of St. Joseph, violet or purple
- of St. Michael, round and blue and black
- of the Seven Dolors of the Blessed Virgin Mary, black
- of the Most Blessed Trinity, white with the blue and red cross of the Trinitarian Order.

A scapular is made of cloth and hangs over the shoulder with a portion in the front and another hanging in the back. The color is distinctive of the order or of the lay apostolate. Some scapulars have pictures and/or prayers imprinted on the cloth while others are simply material. The conferee is invested and receives the scapular in a ceremony that is outlined in the *Book of Blessing,* where the blessing of other sacramentals can be found.

It is recommended that the blessing service be communal and that members of the order or institute be present and participate. Some investitures must be performed by a priest of the order conferring the scapular. Some groups have special ceremonies that supplement the ceremony described in the official *Book of Blessing.*

The ceremony begins with the celebrant greeting the people and reminding them that "through the Son . . . every blessing comes to us from God our Father."

The celebrant may also prepare those in attendance with these or similar words: "This scapular is a sign of entrance into the confraternity of (*name*), approved by the Church. The scapular thus expresses our intention of sharing in the spirit of that Order. That intention renews our baptismal resolve to put on Christ with the help of Mary, whose greatest desire is that we become more like Christ in praise of the Trinity, until, dressed for the wedding feast, we reach our home in heaven."

Then follows the reading of an appropriate Scripture and a homily by the celebrant. Intercessions are prayed that are pertinent to the spirituality of the order or institute and pertain to the needs of those present.

The presider then extends his hands to pray over those who are to be invested with the scapular. "O God . . . look with kindness on those who devoutly receive this scapular. . . . Let them become sharers in the image of Christ. . . ."

The scapular is then placed over the shoulders of the candidates with prayers of conferral that are associated with the nature of the order or institute. The new member then faces those in attendance while the celebrant says: "By being clothed with this scapular you have been accepted into the religious family of (*name*), in order that you may more fully serve Christ and His Church in the spirit of that community. So that you may more completely achieve that goal, I admit you . . . into participation in all the spiritual favors belonging to this religious family."

After sprinkling all present with holy water, the presider gives a concluding prayer and blessing.

The first scapular for use in popular devotion and the one that has been the prototype for other scapulars is the scapular of Our Lady of Mt. Carmel. It is affiliated with the Carmelite Order. According to pious tradition, Our Lady appeared to a Carmelite monk, St. Simon Stock, on July 16, 1251. St. Simon had been praying for deliverance for his order, which was undergoing many trials at the time. Our Lady reportedly gave Simon the brown scapular that is now known as the Scapular of Our Lady of Mt. Carmel. She told Simon that the scapular was to be a sign of her grace to the order and that "whosoever dies clothed in this shall not suffer eternal fire."

Use of this scapular grew considerably in the sixteenth century and adherents to its spirituality continue. Those who accept this scapular pledge to certain observances, mandated by the religious order the scapular symbolizes.

The Blessed Mother has promised her patronage and protection for those who take up this scapular. However, it is not a magic amulet. Some have compared it to a wedding ring — a sign of a promise of two people to love and care for each other. The promise of salvation attached to the scapular must be viewed in this context. The one living a life consecrated to Jesus through Mary will enjoy salvation. The intercession and patronage of the Blessed Mother is of great benefit for the person striving to follow Jesus. Pope Pius XII, while encouraging the devotion, also warns: "But not for this reason (the promise of preservation from hell) . . . may they who wear the scapular think that they can gain salvation while remaining sinful and negligent of spirit, for the apostle warns us: 'In fear and trembling shall you work out your salvation' (Phil 2:12)."

Hold That Thought

Like many devotional practices, the wearing of a scapular is not something necessary for our salvation. Rather, it is another way to grow in love and service of God. It also ensures that we don't walk the road to salvation alone. The prayer and support of fellow faithful Catholics is invaluable to our ability to persevere in the faith and spread the Gospel. Those who join a confraternity of fellow Catholics though investiture of a scapular share in the prayers and good works of all the others who belong to that religious family.

The scapular is also a tangible reminder of the promises and commitments that you have made. Every time you see or feel the scapular you are reminded and called to pray for all those who have made a like consecration.

Items like the scapular are sources of confusion for some non-Catholics. However, when we understand the true meaning and value of these sacramentals they can actually provide a witness. If you wear a scapular, someone will eventually ask: "What is that you are wearing and why do you wear it?" You need to be ready to provide an answer that will point that someone to Jesus.

A Double Witness

"This most extraordinary gift of the scapular from the Mother of God to St. Simon Stock brings its great usefulness not only to the Carmelite Family of Mary but also to all the rest of the Faithful who wish, affiliated to that Family, to follow Mary with a very special devotion."

— Pope Pius IX

"Just as men take pride in having others wear their livery, so the Most Holy Mary is pleased when her servants wear her scapular as a mark that they have dedicated themselves to her service, and are members of the family of the Mother of God."

— St. Alphonsus

"The scapular bears a double witness: to Mary's protection against the ravages of the Flesh occasioned by fall, and to Mary's influence as Mediatrix of Graces, who covers our souls with the richness of her Son's Redemption."

—Bishop Fulton Sheen

"Ever hold in great esteem the practices and exercises of the devotion to the Most Blessed Virgin which have been recommended for centuries by the magisterium of the Church. And among them we judge well to recall especially the Marian Rosary and the religious use of the Scapular of Mt. Carmel."

— Pope Paul VI

How to Wear a Medal

Religious medals are signs of the faith of those who wear them. Normally they are worn on a chain around the neck. As sacramentals they direct our thoughts to the source of all grace, the Lord, Jesus Christ. Like a photograph of a loved one, they remind us of our relationship to God and His saints. Also medals can be a sign of our confidence in the intercession of the Blessed Mother and of the saints. Without a lived faith they are merely pieces of metal. But the man or woman of faith wears a medal as part of a life of prayer and devotion. These medals then become silent prayers reflecting the heart and mind of the wearer.

One of the prayers that a priest or deacon uses in blessing a medal states: "[Lord,] draw near, we pray, to these Your servants and, as they use this symbol of their faith and devotion, grant that they may also strive to be transformed into the likeness of Christ." Thus, each time we see or feel a blessed medal we can confirm that blessing with a silent aspiration: "Lord, transform me!"

There are three formats that a priest or deacon can use to bless a medal, a crucifix, statue or other image. The simplest form requires the minister to make the sign of the cross over the object while praying: "May this (*name of article*) and the one who wears it be blessed, in the name of the Father, and of Son, and of the Holy Spirit. Amen."

One particular medal is more popular than any other. It has become known as the "Miraculous Medal." In 1830 the Blessed Mother appeared to a member of the Daughters of Charity of St. Vincent de Paul. This nun was St. Catherine Labouré. On the second of three apparitions, the Blessed Mother appeared to Catherine standing upon a globe and bearing a globe in her hands. Dazzling rays of light were emanating from her fingers. Catherine saw Mary surrounded by an oval frame. On the frame were the words: "O Mary, conceived without sin, pray for us who have recourse to thee." On the back of this framed vision, Catherine saw the letter M. On top of the letter was a cross. Images of the Sacred Heart of Jesus with a crown of thorns and that of the Heart of Mary pierced with a sword complete the vision on the reverse side.

Mary directed Catherine to have a medal cast in the likeness of the vision and the Blessed Mother promised graces to those who in faith and devotion wore the medal. In 1832 the Archbishop of Paris granted permission for the medals to be made. They were widely distributed, and devotion spread rapidly. One of the most remarkable stories connected with this medal was the conversion of a Jewish man, Alphonse Ratisbonne. He had resisted appeals to join the Catholic Church. However, he reluctantly agreed to wear one of the medals when asked by a friend. Shortly after that, while in Rome, Ratisbonne entered a church and there had a vision of the Blessed Mother as represented on the medal. He converted to the Catholic faith after this incident.

The term "miraculous" over time became the title of the medal. In 1894, Pope Leo XIII approved the devotion and established the feast of the "Manifestation of the Immaculate Virgin under the title of the Miraculous Medal." The feast is celebrated on November 27.

Hold That Thought

The Miraculous Medal has no magic power, nor is it a "good luck" charm. It can be a channel of grace for the prayers and devotions of the faithful. The Miraculous Medal is a testimony of faith and the power of entrusting prayer.

Prayer to Our Lady of the Miraculous Medal

Virgin Mother of God, Mary Immaculate, we unite ourselves to you under your title of Our Lady of the Miraculous Medal. May this medal be for each one of us a sure sign of your motherly affection for us and a constant reminder of our filial duties towards you. While wearing it, may we be blessed by your loving protection and preserved in the grace of your Son. Most powerful Virgin, Mother of our Savior, keep us close to you every moment of our lives so that like you we may live and act according to the teaching and example of your Son. Obtain for us, your children, the grace of a happy death so that in union with you we may enjoy the happiness of heaven forever. Amen. O Mary, conceived without sin, Pray for us who have recourse to you.

Living the Faith

How to Make a "Plan of Life"

Any good business executive will tell you that the best way to succeed is first to establish goals, then develop a plan to reach your goals. That plan involves specific daily steps toward the goal.

This is true in the spiritual life as well, where our goal has already been defined for us. "God draws close to man. He calls man to seek Him, to know Him, to love Him with all his strength. He calls together all men, scattered and divided by sin, into the unity of His family, the Church" (*CCC*, no. 1). We need a spiritual plan — with daily, weekly, monthly, and yearly action steps — that will enable us respond to God Who draws close to us.

Such a program is sometimes called a "plan of life." Here we'll provide a basic list and some general principles:

Prayer
Sacramental life
Spiritual reading
Study of the faith
Spiritual direction
Practice of the Presence of God

Any good plan includes specifics. What must I do

daily to reach my goal? What must I do weekly, monthly, yearly? Consistency is vital. We cannot help but form habits in our everyday life; but habits can be either good or bad. If we form good habits, such as daily prayer or regular study of our faith, these will move us closer to God and His will for our lives.

Thus, in preparing our plan, we should be specific about which devotions, which practices we will fulfill and precisely when we will fulfill them. Whenever possible, we should assign a fixed time for our prayers. If we manage our day using a calendar, appointment book, or pocket computer, we should build prayer into the schedule, just as we would any other appointments.

When we want to succeed at something, we naturally turn to those who have already been successful, and we study what they do. Next, we identify those things that have led to their success. Then we imitate those things consistently. The saints who have gone before us have given us good example of how to grow in a love relationship with God. We should follow their lead, studying the writings and biographies of the saints.

"All Christians in any state or walk of life are called to the fullness of Christian life and to the perfection of charity."
— Vatican Council II, *Lumen Gentium*, no. 31

Hold That Thought

When developing a plan of life, it is important to maintain a balance. Don't try to implement too much all at once. If you have not been praying regularly, it may not be a good idea to start by trying to pray an hour a day. Instead, begin by setting aside fifteen minutes a day — and be faithful to that time. It is better to start small and grow than to attempt something beyond your current ability and become disillusioned. The help of a priest or a mature Catholic lay person can be invaluable as you develop your plan.

While you don't want to set expectations too high, you do want to be committed to the plan you've decided to follow. Let's say that part of your plan includes an hour every Sunday dedicated to reading something that will help you learn more about your faith. You should make every effort to be faithful to that decision, even when it is difficult.

Your plan is a means of reaching a goal. But keep in mind that the essence of that goal is deepening your love relationship with God. Compare this love with other relationships in your life — your relationship with your spouse, good friends, co-workers, and so on. In each case, you need to devote time and energy to help the relationship grow. Sometimes that means sacrifice: you must, for example, turn off the television or forgo some other activity in order to spend time with the other person. It's no different with God.

Make a Plan

"Sow an act, reap a habit.
Sow a habit, reap a character.
Sow a character, reap a destiny."

— Anonymous

"Let us listen to Our Lord: 'He who is faithful in a very little thing is faithful also in much; and he who is dishonest in a very little thing is dishonest also in much.' It is as if He were saying to us: 'Fight continuously in the apparently unimportant things which are to My mind important; fulfill your duty punctually; smile at whoever needs cheering up, even though there is sorrow in your soul; devote the necessary time to prayer, without haggling.' "

— Blessed Josémaria Escrivá

"How easily you leave the plan of life unfinished, or do things so badly that it is worse than not doing them at all. Is that the way you mean to fall in love more each day with your way, and to pass on this love later to others?"

— Blessed Josémaria Escrivá

"May He give you a humble love which expends itself;
a generous love which forgets itself;
a strong love which is not afraid of pain;
a stable love which does not change;
a patient love which never weakens;
a constant love which never falters."

— Blessed Mother Mary Angela Truszkowska

How to Keep
the Presence of God

One of the most popular Christian books of all time is a little volume called *The Practice of the Presence of God.* It was written by a seventeenth-century monk, Brother Lawrence. Christians have been fascinated through the centuries at how this simple, uneducated man developed such a close relationship with God. Brother Lawrence writes: "When we are faithful to keep ourselves in His holy Presence, and set Him always before us, this not only hinders our offending Him . . . but it also begets in us a holy freedom, and if I may so speak, a familiarity with God. In fine, by often repeating these acts, they become habitual, and the presence of God is rendered, as it were, natural to us."

Brother Lawrence saw clearly that God is always with us. We too can have a lived experience of the presence of God. We need first to grow in our understanding of God and His work among us; then we need to make active decisions to unite ourselves to God through prayers and works of love, adoration, service, and the like. The first step we will accomplish through our sustained study and prayer. The second step we can achieve by various methods of "prayer of the presence of God."

Now, how do you practically accomplish this amid daily distractions and obligations? Begin each day with a morning offering in which you state your desire to walk with Christ throughout the day, doing everything according to His will and pleasure. Then, during the day, seek to turn your heart toward God regularly. You can do this by mentally praying a short prayer (aspiration) or merely turning your heart to Him with loving affection.

Some Christians key their aspirations to different

events: Some commuters pray every time they reach a traffic light. Some office workers use a ringing phone as a reminder to offer a quick prayer. Still others offer an aspiration whenever their digital wristwatch beeps the hour. All these things can help us to keep constantly aware of the presence of God.

We will notice real benefits from this practice. First, knowing that God is with us can help us to avoid sin and resist temptation. It can also help us to grow in virtue. We always strive to act our best when we are in the company of important people: the boss or the person we love most. This is true to a much greater degree when we realize that we are in the company of God.

A second method of keeping the presence of God is to consciously offer each and every task to God as an Act of Love. If our employer gives us an assignment at work, we can ask God to help us work in a way that will please our employer, even as it serves the divine will.

Hold That Thought

As with many areas of the spiritual life, this is a lifelong journey. If we are faithful to our practice of aspirations, we can, over time, continually grow in our awareness of God's presence. Progress will depend upon a humble attitude that seeks God's assistance, coupled with a commitment that is regularly renewed.

Religious images can also be helpful. A small cross at our workstation or hung on the refrigerator can be a silent reminder. A rosary in your pocket or purse, where you will regularly see it or feel it, can serve the same purpose. Whenever you see or feel the cross or the beads, you can turn your heart and mind to God and tell Him that you love Him.

The Presence of God

"It is possible while sitting in your workshop stitching leather to consecrate your heart to God. It is possible . . . for the person standing over a pot cooking to make fervent and frequent prayer, even though it is not possible to enter a church. For God takes no thought of place. This alone He requires of us: a mind and soul that love the things of God."

— St. John Chrysostom

"I have been crucified with Christ; it is no longer I who live, but Christ who lives in me; and the life I now live in the flesh I live by faith in the Son of God, Who loved me and gave Himself for me."

— Galatians 2:19-20

"Pray at all times in the Spirit."

— Ephesians 6:18

"Do everything as though you really saw His Majesty before you; by acting thus a soul gains greatly."

— St. Teresa of Jesus

"If we keep ourselves always in the presence of God, the thought that He sees all our thoughts, that He hears our words and observes all our actions will preserve us from thinking any evil, from speaking any evil, and from doing any evil."

— St. John Chrysostom

Psalm 139

Whither shall I go from Thy Spirit?
　　or whither shall I flee from Thy presence?
If I ascend to heaven, Thou art there!
　　If I make my bed in Sheol, Thou art there!
If I take the wings of the morning
　　and dwell in the uttermost parts of the sea,
even there Thy hand shall lead me,
　　and Thy right hand shall hold me.
If I say, "Let only darkness cover me,
　　and the light about me be night,"
even the darkness is not dark to Thee,
　　the night is bright as the day;
　　for darkness is as light with Thee.

Psalm 139:7-12

Prayer to Keep the Presence of God

Lord, God Almighty, You have brought me safely to the beginning of this new day. Defend me today by Your mighty power, so that I may not fall into any sin, and that all my words may so proceed and all my thoughts and actions be so directed as to be always just in Your sight. Through Christ my Lord. Amen.

How to Witness to the Faith

Someone has said that to be a Christian is to be on "mission." The key in devotion to Christ is obedience, and Jesus told His disciples to go and make disciples of all nations. So there is no doubt about our obligation to preach the Gospel and witness to the faith.

Vatican Council II emphasized the role of the laity in the Church. Lay people are called not only to a life of holiness but also to the task of taking Christ into the world. *Lumen Gentium*, one of the documents of Vatican II states: "The laity are called in a special way to make the Church present and operative in those places and circumstances where only through them can it become the salt of the earth. Thus every layman, in virtue of the very gifts bestowed upon him, is at the same time a witness and a living instrument of the mission of the Church" (no. 33).

How are we to fulfill our mission of bringing the Gospel to the world? First we must be striving to live a Christian life. This does not mean that we need to be perfect "saints" before we begin to witness. It does mean that our own lives need to be committed to God and His ways. Most people can accept that we are struggling to live Christian lives. But they will never accept the Good News from someone who is not striving to live it.

We should also be involved in what Cardinal Newman called "the apostolate of personal influence." We all have a circle of people with whom we share our lives: family, work, professional organizations, neighbors, and social groups. Our example and our friendships can be a great channel for the grace of God to work in people's lives.

Our friendships need to be sincere. We don't want to make a friend so that we can then make a "conquest" for the faith. Rather we make friends out of a genuine concern for people and to follow the example of love displayed by our Savior. With friends we will talk about sports, what the kids are doing, our thoughts on various issues and, when appropriate, what we do as a Catholic. This should not be done in a pushy manner. Religion doesn't need to be included in every conversation. But in a strong friendship we will be talking about all the life situations that are important to us and so we will naturally include our faith.

We should identify a person or persons with whom we particularly hope to share the Gospel. Then — and this may be the most important element — we need to pray for those individuals in a dedicated way, asking the Holy Spirit to work in their hearts and draw them closer to Christ. We need the wisdom and love of Christ as we reach out to others, so we also should ask God's grace to be instruments to help these people find Christ.

Friendship, good example, and prayer are all important but, as the Scripture points out, people must "hear" the Word. At some point we should raise the question with our friends: "Have you ever considered becoming a Catholic?" We want to share what is most precious to us with those we love and we have nothing more precious than our faith. This type of question, asked in the context of a relationship, will not be offensive to people. You can get a variety of responses. Some will not want to talk about the issue at that time, but may want to discuss it at some later time.

"It is terrible how much harm we can do if we allow ourselves to be carried away by the fear or the shame of being seen as Christians in ordinary life."

— **Blessed Josémaria Escrivá**

When individuals show interest, we must help them to take the next steps. You can invite them to accompany you to Mass. Good Catholic literature is invaluable as a tool to introduce people to the faith. It is important to be open to their questions. Put them in contact with a priest and encourage them to take steps forward in investigating the faith. Pray with them. Perhaps invite them to join your family in some faith activity.

Remember that you are God's instrument. That will help you to keep a good perspective. Knowing that it is the Holy Spirit who brings people to conversion will keep you from being too pushy. But realizing that God calls you to this work with this individual should give you confidence. If a particular person is your friend, it is safe to say that God desires you to influence that person for his/her spiritual good.

Consider This

"On Evangelization in the Modern World" (*Evangelii Nuntiandi* is the Latin title) is one of the encyclicals of Pope Paul VI. It provides a worthy overview of the call to proclaim the Good News. It is both practical and inspirational — well worth your time to read.

One of the greatest blessings for a Catholic is to be able to share your faith with others and see them respond to Christ. It builds your own faith. And a friend who comes to share your faith is a friend indeed to be cherished.

"You catch more flies with a little honey than with a barrel of vinegar."

— St. Francis de Sales

Go Ye Therefore . . .

"There is no true evangelization if the name, the teaching, the life, the promises, the kingdom and the mystery of Jesus of Nazareth, the Son of God are not proclaimed."
— **Pope Paul VI**, *Evangelii Nuntiandi*, no. 22

"In the long run, is there any other way of handing on the Gospel than by transmitting to another person one's personal experience of faith?"
—**Pope Paul VI**, *Evangelii Nuntiandi*, no. 46

"Lay people, whose particular vocation places them in the midst of the world and in charge of the most varied temporal tasks, must for this very reason exercise a very special form of evangelization."
— **Pope Paul VI**, *Evangelii Nuntiandi*, no. 70

"Jesus Christ alone has shed the Blood that redeems the world. Alone, too, He might have put its power to work and acted directly, as He does in the Holy Eucharist. But He wanted to have others cooperate in the distribution of His graces. Why? No doubt His Divine Majesty demanded that it be so, but His loving affection for men urged Him no less. And if it is seemly for the most excellent king to govern, more often than not, through ministers, what condescension it is for God to deign to give poor creatures a share in His work and His glory."
— **Pope Leo XIII**

"We exhort the laity: Christian families, youth, adults, all those who exercise a trade or profession, leaders, without forgetting the poor who are often rich in faith and hope—all lay people who are conscious of their evangelizing role in the service of their Church or in the midst of society and the world. We say to all of them: our evangelizing zeal must spring from true holiness of life, and, as the Second Vatican Council suggests, preaching must in its turn make the preacher grow in holiness, which is nourished by prayer and above all by love for the Eucharist."

— **Pope Paul VI,** *Evangelii Nuntiandi,* **no. 76**

"The Christian community is never closed in upon itself. The intimate life of this community — the life of listening to the Word and the apostles' teaching, charity lived in a fraternal way, the sharing of bread — this intimate life only acquires its full meaning when it becomes a witness, when it evokes admiration and conversion, and when it becomes the preaching and proclamation of the Good News. Thus it is the whole Church that receives the mission to evangelize, and the work of each individual member is important for the whole."

— **Pope Paul VI,** *Evangelii Nuntiandi,* **no. 15**

How to Begin
Spiritual Direction

Progress in the spiritual life can be difficult. Temptations arise from within us. We resist the struggles to grow closer to God because we desire the easy path. It is easy to become blind to our faults and to deceive ourselves concerning our spiritual progress. Pride and other vices can blind us.

And the devil doesn't want us to progress in our relationship with God. The evil one will do his best to tempt and deceive us.

Moreover we get very little support in our quest for holiness from the world around us: "Live for today!" "Grab all the gusto you can get!" These are not themes that lead us on the road to Christ. Our modern culture provides its own sources of temptation: sensuality, materialism, etc.

Meanwhile, if we are striving to live for Christ, we desire to overcome the patterns of sin in our lives. We want to be faithful to the plan of life we established to help us grow spiritually, and we want to witness to Christ. The sacraments are an immense help in our struggles against "the world, the flesh, and the devil," but is there more that we can do?

The Sacrament of Confession is a great source of help in overcoming sin. In the confessional the priest may point out ways to avoid our sins and improve. Or he may give us insight into the true nature of our sin and suggest ways to make amends and grow. However, this is a fairly passive approach on our part. We confess our sins and then leave it up to the priest to discern any advice he might give. There is a way to be more actively involved in the process: we can seek Spiritual direction.

Spiritual direction is an ongoing, long-term dialogue

that involves three individuals: the spiritual director, the individual receiving direction, and the Holy Spirit. The intent is to provide private guidance to the individual in accordance with his or her unique spiritual needs. The director seeks to help us to grow in the Christian life, with the goal of perfection in Christ, in accordance with our state of life. For the lay person, then, the director seeks to move us toward faithfulness in the vocation of marriage or in life as single persons. Spiritual direction helps us to cultivate virtues and be watchful against faults and spiritual dangers.

Ordinarily, we will seek spiritual direction from a priest, although a deacon or trained lay person can also do the job. One way to begin is to identify a priest who can be a regular confessor, then ask him if he would provide spiritual direction. A session every four weeks is usually adequate for spiritual direction, unless there is a pressing need for more frequent guidance.

There are two specific topics you will want to focus on in spiritual direction. One is the root sin you are striving to overcome. Here you should be specific. It is of little help to tell the director: "I've been proud" without saying how and when.

The second topic is how well you are fulfilling the duties of your state in life. How are you functioning as a Christian wife and mother, or husband and father? How are you doing in your plan of life (the practical steps you are taking to grow closer to God)? What difficulties have you encountered? What progress have you made? Are you being faithful to your promises and spiritual resolutions?

The spiritual director will talk with you about these issues, ask questions, and provide practical suggestions for improvement. Remember that there are three parties in this endeavor, and the Holy Spirit is at the heart of the relationship. The Holy Spirit desires to shed light on both the director and you who are seeking the guidance. So be open and forthright in the discussion. In the resulting conversation, you and your director can discern in very concrete ways what will impact your daily life.

Normally the director will discuss resolutions with you. These are specific commitments that you make to amend some part of your life. You can also make them part of your daily examination of conscience. You should make an accounting of your progress to your director at your next session.

For example, after discussion with your spiritual director, you may commit to be more faithful to Morning Prayer, since you have often skipped it. Also, since you have been short tempered with your wife, you may resolve to take certain specific steps to improve here, perhaps resolving to leave work concerns at the office and arrive home cheerful and focused on the needs of your spouse.

Then, day to day, you will seek to implement consistent Morning Prayer and the specific ways you have decided to improve your relationship with your wife. Each night, when you examine your conscience, review these areas. When you again meet with the spiritual director, you will report on your progress. From this report the spiritual director can help you to further improve.

Other topics may be discussed with your spiritual director. For example, what is the general state of your soul and your relationship with God? Are you experiencing dryness, distraction, or preoccupation during prayer? Or are you calm, peaceful, confident, and experiencing God's grace?

You can also discuss your Christian outreach with your director. What are you doing to witness and serve as a Christian? Do you live with a spirit of faith, hope, and love? What sacrifices and mortifications do you practice? What are your ultimate intentions — the glory of God and the building of His kingdom or personal satisfactions and the esteem of others?

Submitting to spiritual direction also can be invaluable in the formation of your conscience. The director can help you avoid both scrupulosity and rationalization. Ultimately, spiritual direction can draw you closer to God and make you a more effective servant of others.

Hold That Thought

When looking for a spiritual director, you should take time in considering your choice. You want a person who is mature spiritually and experienced in direction. With a priest you can combine your spiritual direction with sacramental confession.

However, you will never find a "perfect" director. Perfect directors don't exist because there are no perfect people on this side of heaven! But if you combine a dedicated spiritual director with an attitude of prayer, humility, and openness on your part and then add the guidance of the Holy Spirit, great progress can be made in the spiritual life.

Growing Closer to God

"Whoever makes himself his own master in the spiritual life, makes himself the student of a fool."

— St. Bernard

"There is no vice which makes it so easy for the devil to drag down to death and eternal ruin souls consecrated to God as this desire to shape our own course independently and to dispense with the counsels of enlightened men."

— Cassian

"The spiritual life is first of all a life. It is not merely something to be known and studied, it is to be lived."

— Thomas Merton

"No one can judge oneself impartially; we have to know ourselves, but at the same time we must not lose courage. It is this balance that the faithful Catholic obtains from spiritual direction."

— François Mauriac

"Certainly, 'spiritual direction' can be carried out even outside the Sacrament of Penance and even by someone who is not endowed with Holy Orders. In this way the penitent overcomes the danger of arbitrariness. . . ."

— Pope John Paul II

How to Do
"Spiritual Reading"

When we discussed mental prayer in a previous chapter, we said that a spiritual book can be of help in beginning to pray. The practice of spiritual reading has value in itself and creates in us an attitude of prayer and receptivity to God. The material we read in spiritual books has been compared to the oil in a lamp. As the oil is the fuel to keep the wick burning, so spiritual reading is the "fuel" that helps keep the spiritual fires burning as we go to prayer.

Spiritual reading has also been compared to food. It provides nourishment for the soul that strengthens us in our relationship with God. Paul follows this theme when he says we need to go beyond "milk" to "solid food" in our spiritual lives (see Heb 5:12-13). The reading of holy books gives us solid food for the enrichment of souls.

There are several categories of spiritual reading that we can consider. First the Bible, especially the New Testament, should be regular, daily reading material for the Christian. It is the divinely inspired word of God. As we begin to read we should ask the same Spirit who inspired the writer to inspire us, the reader, as we take up the Holy Word of God. Choose an approved modern version for your reading. The *New American Bible* is the scriptural version on which the readings at Mass are based in the United States. The *Jerusalem Bible* has been used in some other English-speaking countries, such as England and Australia. The *Revised Standard Version, Catholic Edition,* is a slightly older translation that has a poetic beauty. Scripture should become so much a part of us that key passages come to our minds as we think about life situations. There are also commentaries that assist in the prayerful reading of Scripture.

Next there are classical spiritual works by saints such as St. Teresa of Ávila, St. Francis de Sales, John of the Cross, St. Ignatius of Loyola, and others. Some of these may be difficult reading for those who are newer in the spiritual life.

There are many works by more recent spiritual writers that are helpful for the average reader. Most of these writers base their material on the writings of the spiritual masters (the saints mentioned above) but put them into a format and language that is more understandable to the modern reader. However, discernment and direction are often helpful because there are also many books that are *not* helpful for the Catholic who wishes to grow in accordance with the teaching of the Catholic faith and the wisdom of the saints.

Finally, the reading of the lives of the saints can provide helpful spiritual inspiration. These books provide lived examples of the truths and principles that are discussed in other spiritual works of literature. As mentioned above, discernment is needed in select books in this category. There are many very good biographies available but there are also some that are not worth the time and energy. Some older lives of the saints indulged in a sentimentality that is not inspiring to the modern reader. Some modern works focus on revisionist history or on the psychological aspects of the saint's life rather that on the relationship of the saint to God.

"You will find none in earnest about his spiritual progress who does not give time to spiritual reading."

— **St. Athanasius**

You don't want to approach a book for spiritual devotion in the same way that you would approach a novel. You want to approach spiritual reading prayerfully. Ask for the guidance of the Holy Spirit, and open your heart and mind to God and His grace so that the reading will be formative. Most spiritual works should be read slowly and reflectively and in small segments so that the contents can be "digested." Key points from your spiritual reading can be used in your meditative prayer.

Consider This

Below we have listed a few books for spiritual reading. The list is *far* from exhaustive. It is only meant to give you a few selections to consider. It is a good practice to ask your spiritual director or a mature Catholic friend to recommend a good spiritual book. Then, as you read, review your progress with your spiritual director.

This Tremendous Lover by Dom Eugene Boylan is considered a modern classic in spiritual reading. Father Boylan also wrote *Difficulties in Mental Prayer.*

The Story of a Soul is the autobiography of St. Thérèse of Lisieux. Her "little way" has inspired many.

Introduction to the Devout Life by St. Francis de Sales was written in another time but continues to inspire today. It is considered a classic for lay spirituality.

The Fire Within by Fr. Thomas DuBay, S.M., is a rather recent book. It makes the spirituality of St. John of the Cross and St. Teresa of Ávila accessible to the modern reader.

To Know Christ Jesus by Frank Sheed will lead you to look at Christ, His life, and His call with a fresh perspective.

He Leadeth Me by Father Walter J. Ciszek, S.J., chronicles the author's life while imprisoned in Communist Russia for the faith. Although he is not a canonized saint, his cause is being considered by the Church.

In Conversation With God is a series of seven books that provides reflections based on the Church's liturgical year. It was written by Francis Fernandez.

The *Navarre Scripture Commentary* is available in a series of twelve books. These books provide the *Revised Standard Version* of the New Testament books with commentary drawn from the Fathers of the Church, the writings of the saints, and from papal documents.

Holiness for Housewives is by Dom Hubert Van Zeller. Although focusing on homemakers, this book is of value to all men and women.

My Daily Bread was written in the 1950s by Father Anthony Panaone, S.J. The reflections on the spiritual life are broken into small segments for daily reading. The small size of the book makes it easy to fit in a purse or vest pocket for reading on the bus.

Solid Food

"When we pray we speak to God, and when we read good books; God speaks to us."

— St. Ambrose

"To a spiritual life, the reading of holy books is perhaps not less useful than mental prayer. St. Bernard says reading instructs us at once in prayer, and in the practice of virtue. Hence he concludes that spiritual reading and prayer are the arms by which hell is conquered and paradise won."

— St. Alphonsus Liguori

Prayer Before Beginning Spiritual Reading

Come, Holy Spirit, fill the hearts of Your faithful, and enkindle in them the Fire of Your Love. Send forth Your Spirit, and they shall be created;

R. And You shall renew the face of the earth.

Let us pray.

O God, Who by the Light of the Holy Spirit did instruct the hearts of Your faithful, grant us in that same Spirit to be truly wise and ever to rejoice in His consolations, through Christ Our Lord. Amen.

How to Study the Faith

Health and diet books are always on the bestseller list. Good health is obviously important enough that people are willing to buy the latest book so that they will know how to live in order to maintain good health. People in business attend seminars and classes to keep on top of their particular field of expertise. They know that continuous training is necessary if they are to remain competitive. People still buy secular newspapers and magazines or go on line so that they can know the latest news. Golf and tennis classes at the local "Y" or community center are almost always full. Computer training, self-help groups, and community college classes all receive enough registrations that they continue to be offered. Many of these learning activities are expensive, but people seem willing to pay the price because they desire to learn and grow.

Since all the above is true, it seems reasonable to assume that diocesan and regional educational events, parish classes, Bible studies, and Catholic magazines and bookstores would also be doing a booming business. However, in most instances this is not the case. In fact many large parishes are happy if a dozen people attend the weekly Lenten lecture series.

The Church has always stressed that the intellectual pursuit of the truth is essential to the life of faith. Pope John Paul II addressed this issue in his 1998 encyclical "Faith and Reason" (*Fides et Ratio*). He began the encyclical by pointing out that "faith and reason are like two wings on which the human spirit rises to the contemplation of the truth."

We are made of body, mind, and spirit. Each component needs proper nourishment in order for us to function as healthy, integrated individuals. If we take reasonable

> "Understanding is the reward of the Faith."
>
> — **St. Augustine**

---

care of our physical being, our good bodily health will assist us in both mental and spiritual activity. On the other hand, if people were only concerned about their physical condition with no concern about the other aspects of life, we rightly would say that such individuals lacked balance.

Our spiritual life needs the nourishment of the sacraments and of prayer — topics that we have been discussing in this book. Our intellects need the nourishment of training in truth and beauty. The *Catechism of the Catholic Church* tells us that when we grow in faith it helps us to better understand the world, while when we obtain "a more penetrating knowledge" it will "call forth a greater faith" (no. 158) that will set our hearts afire with the love of God. St. Augustine writes: "I believe, in order to understand; and I understand, the better to believe."

As our faith in God grows, and as we experience God's love and providential working in the world, our eyes of faith are opened to new reality. We take this faith life with us when we study the principles of our faith. We then see the truth both with new eyes and with a new level of understanding. Truth better understood gives us a deeper knowledge of God and of human nature which, in turn, serves to increase our faith and love of God.

This is the way growth occurs. It is like climbing a ladder where the rungs alternate between faith and intellectual understanding. The result is that as we climb we make progress toward Him Who is the source of all truth, God Himself.

We can't rely only upon the knowledge of our faith that we obtained through a grade-school program or through an RCIA series. If our faith has been growing, our understanding also needs to accompany that growth. The reward of our pursuit of understanding is an ever-increasing reservoir of material for the development of our faith and love of God.

There are many methods we can use in studying our Catholic faith. We can take advantage of structured learning programs that are available locally through our parish or diocese. Several Catholic colleges and institutes also offer extension classes where you can participate in a structured learning program in the convenience of your home.

The wonders of modern technology have made information available to us in convenient media. There are audio and videotapes that bring the teaching of Catholic scholars into your car or living room. More educational material is now being made available over the Internet as well. In addition there are many good Catholic magazines and books that can be read according to your schedule.

There are a variety of subjects that the Catholic should explore in developing a better understanding of the faith. First, we should become better versed in the Scriptures. We read the Bible as a source of prayer, but we also should read it as a source of knowledge about God and His ways. The Bible is a foundational gift from God, so shouldn't we make it a goal to read all of it? There are many commentaries that can be used to assist our understanding of the texts. A better understanding of Bible history will increase both our understanding and appreciation of the original text.

In addition, we should read official Church texts. Re-

"Nothing is more excellent than knowledge."
— St. John of Damascus

255

cent popes have written encyclicals on a wide variety of subjects. Some are more intellectually challenging than others. For example, "Faith and Reason" is not light reading. Pope John Paul II's "Letter to Families" is something we can all read and appreciate. Don't be discouraged if you struggle with a particular document. Search out material that is understandable yet stretches you, too.

A particular blessing for our generation is the *Catechism of the Catholic Church* which was first released in 1994. Every Catholic home should have a copy of the *Catechism*. It is not the type of book that you may want to read cover to cover but it provides an invaluable resource. If a question arises on a particular topic, you can look in the appropriate section of the *Catechism*.

St. Peter counsels us to "always be prepared to make a defense to any one who calls you to account for the hope that is in you, yet do it with gentleness and reverence" (1 Pt 3:15). Apologetics is the defense or explanation of your reasons for your faith. In order to make that defense or give that explanation, you need to both know the faith and be comfortable in speaking about it. There are many books that can assist you.

Another area of study that should be on the list of every Catholic reading program is history. Start with a book that details the life of Christ. Goodier, Sheen, and Guardini have all written excellent volumes. Follow up with a history of the Church (we recommend some at the end of this book).

The Fathers of the Church and the writings of the saints (such as Augustine and Thomas Aquinas) are available in modern translations. These testimonies from historical figures provide a sense of continuity in the faith.

Consider This

Discernment is needed in selecting material for the study of the faith. First make sure that the book, tape, or class is faithful to the teaching of the faith. Also choose material that you will understand. While it is good to undertake material that provides a mental challenge, material that is too academic may discourage you in the long haul.

Another suggestion is to ask a couple of Catholic friends to join you in reading a particular book. Make a schedule that will require a certain portion to be read each week. Then once a week join with your Catholic friends and share your thoughts on what you have read. This team approach has helped many to be consistent in a reading program that increases the knowledge of their faith while building relationships that are based upon a shared belief.

Learn and Grow

"Anything that pits faith against reason, belief against knowledge, or religious experience against critical intelligence has no place in authentically Christian thought."

— Richard Neuhaus

"Let us read with method, and propose to ourselves an end to what our studies may point. The use of reading is to aid us in thinking."

— Edward Gibbon

How to Pray for the Pope

In the Gospel of John, Jesus appears to the disciples and He speaks to Peter. He confirms Peter in the office of leader of the fledgling Church. Peter is commanded and empowered to "feed the sheep" that belong to the Good Shepherd. As Jesus calls Peter to "follow me," He also warns Peter that there will be suffering in following Him and in leading the Church in the office of the first pope (see Jn 21:15-19).

The pope is called the "Vicar of Christ." A vicar is one who serves in the place of another, and so the pope serves the Church in the place of Christ. Just as Christ suffered, our Holy Father too suffers rejection and betrayal. The pope proclaims the truth in love to a hurting world, yet he is often ignored or ridiculed. Even within the Church our Holy Father suffers because of misunderstanding and abandonment. The Holy Father, as the Vicar of Christ, daily walks a road of Calvary. Pope St. Leo the Great rightly called the papacy a "burden."

The Holy Father needs men and women, who, like Simon of Cyrene (Lk 23:26), will help him to bear the cross — a cross that is meant to bring blessing and life to the world. The first Christians understood that the best way to the pope is prayer. When Herod imprisoned Peter, we are told, "earnest prayer was made to God by the church" (Acts 12:5). We, too, need to support the Holy Father by our regular, earnest prayer.

History shows that our prayers for the pope are effective. The result of the Church's prayer for Peter was his miraculous release from prison. Our prayers for the Holy Father will be heard and answered today as well.

During the Eucharistic Prayer at each Mass, we can join with the priest as he prays for the pope. We should then follow the example of the early Church and include

258

the Holy Father in our daily prayers of intercession, especially remembering to pray for his health and protection.

We should foster a prayer concern for those particular intentions that are important to the pope. The pontiff knows the needs of the Church, and he carries them in his heart and mind. St. Peter himself tells us that there is a blessing for us when we are of "one mind" (see 1 Pt 3:8-9). Our Lord assures us that when we agree together in prayer, He will hear and answer (see Mt 18:19-20).

The Apostleship of Prayer is a ministry that promotes prayer among the laity. Each month the Apostleship publishes two of the intentions of the pope, and asks for the faithful to pray daily for those intentions. One of these intentions is "general" and may concern any one of a number of needs or problems that face the Church. The second intention is a "missionary intention" and focuses on some aspect of the call to proclaim the Good News of Jesus to the world. Pope John Paul II has spoken of the immense significance of these monthly intentions. Some Catholic periodicals and parish bulletins make the prayer intentions available. The intentions can also be obtained on a number of Catholic websites including the website of the Apostleship of Prayer (www.cin.org/ap).

The Apostleship suggests the daily recitation of a decade of the Rosary for the special intentions of the Holy Father that are recommended each month.

Consider This

We need to strive to have the heart and mind of the Church. When we pray regularly for the intentions of the Church, as embodied in the intentions of the Holy Father, our heart and mind will resemble more closely the heart and mind of the Church — and therefore the heart and mind of Christ Himself. Thus our prayers can assist the pope, further the work of the Church, and form us as disciples of Christ.

Prayers for the Pope

Let us pray for our Most Holy Father, *Pope N.* May the Lord preserve him and give him life, and make him blessed upon the earth, and deliver him not up to the will of his enemies. Amen.

Traditional Prayer

Lord, source of eternal life and truth, give to your shepherd *Pope N.* a spirit of courage and right judgment, a spirit of knowledge and love. By governing with fidelity those entrusted to his care may he, as successor to the apostle Peter and vicar of Christ, build your Church into a sacrament of unity, love, and peace for all the world. We ask this through Our Lord Jesus Christ, your Son, Who lives and reigns with you and the Holy Spirit, one God forever and ever. Amen.

— From the Roman Missal

The Vicar of Christ

"How can I do it?"

— Pope Pius XII

"Where Peter is, there is the Church."

— St. Ambrose of Milan

"Have pity on me!"

— Pope Paul VI, upon his election

Where to Learn More

A Beginning

Guardini, Romano, *The Art of Praying* (Sophia Institute Press).

How I Pray Now, James Manney, editor (Our Sunday Visitor).

A Plan of Life (Scepter Booklets).

Catholic Prayers

Fox, Fr. Robert J., *A Catholic Prayer* Book (Our Sunday Visitor, 1974).

Guardini, Romano, *The Lord's Prayer* (Sophia Institute Press).

Handbook of Prayers, Rev. James Socias, editor (Our Sunday Visitor, 1997).

Traditional Catholic Prayers, Msgr. Charles J. Dollen, editor (Our Sunday Visitor, 1990).

A Tradition of Prayer

Boylan, Eugene, *Difficulties in Mental Prayer* (Scepter Press).

Garant, Sandra Schuck, *Living in Prayer* (Pauline Books & Media).

Miller, Rev. J. Michael, C.S.B., *Praying for the Dead* (Our Sunday Visitor, 1994).

Salvail, Ghislaine, *At the Crossroads of the Scriptures* (Pauline Books & Media).

Praying with Mary

Dollen, Msgr. Charles, *Listen, Mother of God!* (Our Sunday Visitor, 1989).

Figari, Luis Fernando, *With Mary in Prayer* (Our Sunday Visitor, 1999).

Gribble, Richard, C.S.C., *The History and Devotion of the Rosary* (Our Sunday Visitor, 1992).

Hammes, John A., Ph.D., *One-Month Scriptural Rosary* (Our Sunday Visitor, 1999).

Penitential Devotions

Baur, Benedict, *Frequent Confession* (Lumen Christi Press, 1984).

Crowley, Rev. John A., *A Day With the Lord: Volume 3, Lent and Eastertide* (Our Sunday Visitor).

Pope John Paul II, *The Mercy of God* (Pauline Books & Media).

St. John Fisher, *Exposition of the Seven Penitential Psalms* (Ignatius Press).

Eucharistic Devotions

Belmonte, Charles, *Understanding the Mass* (Scepter Press).

Groeschel, Fr. Benedict J., C.F.R., *Praying in the Presence of Our Lord* (Our Sunday Visitor, 1999).

Guardini, Romano, *Meditations before Mass* (Sophia Institute Press, 1993).

Hahn, Scott, *The Lamb's Supper: The Mass as Heaven on Earth* (Doubleday, 1999).

Mauriac, Francois, *Holy Thursday* (Sophia Institute Press, 1991).

Sacramentals and Blessings

Ball, Ann, *A Handbook of Catholic Sacramentals* (Our Sunday Visitor, 1991).

Catholic Household Blessings and Prayers, U.S. Bishops' Committee on the Liturgy (United States Catholic Conference).

Dubruiel, Michael, *(Mention Your Request Here), The Church's Most Powerful Novenas* (Our Sunday Visitor, 2000).

Favorite Prayers and Novenas, compiled by the Daughters of St. Paul (Pauline Books & Media).

The Stations of the Cross, a Video with Bishop Donald W. Wuerl (Our Sunday Visitor).

Welborn, Amy and Dubruiel, Michael, *The Biblical Way of the Cross* (Ave Maria Press).

Living the Faith /
Witness to the Faith

Berlucchi, Jim, *Person to Person* (Servant Books, 1984).
McCloskey, C. John, *Winning Converts* (Scepter Booklets, 1997).

Spiritual Reading

Hughes, Bishop Alfred, *Spiritual Masters* (Our Sunday Visitor, 1998).

Studying the Faith

Aquilina, Mike, *The Fathers of the Church* (Our Sunday Visitor, 1999).
Aquilina, Mike and Fr. Kris Stubna, *What Catholics Believe* (Our Sunday Visitor, 1999).
Bunson, Matthew and Margaret, *Encyclopedia of Catholic History,* (Our Sunday Visitor).
Martin, George, *God's Word* (Our Sunday Visitor, 1998).
McBride, Alfred O.Praem., *Father McBride's Family Catechism* and *Father McBride's Teen Catechism* (Our Sunday Visitor).
The Teaching of Christ, Fourth Edition, Bishop Donald Wuerl et al., editors (Our Sunday Visitor, 1995).

About the Authors

MIKE AQUILINA is best known as the editor of *New Covenant* magazine and as an award-winning Catholic writer. A prolific author, his latest book, the bestseller *What Catholics Believe*, coauthored by Fr. Kris D. Stubna, sold more than 10,000 copies in less than a year. His other books include *Talking to Youth About Sexuality, Weapons of the Spirit* (with Dave Scott), and *The Fathers of the Church*. Mike, his wife, Terri, and their four children live in Pennsylvania.

REGIS FLAHERTY is a widely published author in the Catholic press. Formerly Executive Director of the Catholic Cemeteries Association of the Diocese of Pittsburgh, the Archdiocese of Boston Catholic Cemeteries, and the Diocese of Tucson, Regis is currently a consultant to Catholic cemetery organizations. Regis and his wife, Libbie, are also Pennsylvania residents with four children.

Other Books
by Mike Aquilina

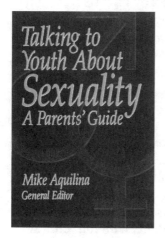

Talking to Youth About Sexuality. A guide for faith-filled parents who want to provide their children with Christian education in sexuality and the family.

0-87973-**716**-6, paper, $3.95, 64 pp.

Biographies of twenty-five of the leading Fathers of the Church, including Clement, Justin Martyr, Ambrose, Jerome, and Augustine.

0-97973-**689**-5, paper, $10.95, 240 pp.

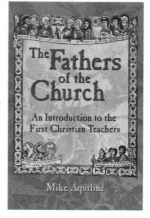

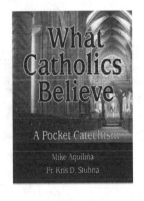